The Autism and Neurodiversity
Self-Advocacy Handbook

by the same author

Spectrum Women
Walking to the Beat of Autism
Edited by Barb Cook and Dr Michelle Garnett
Foreword by Lisa Morgan
ISBN 978 1 78592 434 7
eISBN 978 1 78450 806 7

The Awesome Autistic Go-To Guide
A Practical Handbook for Autistic Teens and Tweens
Yenn Purkis and Tanya Masterman
Foreword by Dr Emma Goodall
ISBN 978 1 78775 316 7
eISBN 978 1 78775 317 4

The Autistic Trans Guide to Life
Yenn Purkis and Wenn Lawson
Foreword by Dr Emma Goodall
ISBN 978 1 78775 391 4
eISBN 978 1 78775 392 1

of related interest

The #ActuallyAutistic Guide to Advocacy
Step-by-Step Advice on How to Ally and Speak Up with
Autistic People and the Autism Community
Jennifer Brunton and Jenna Gensic
ISBN 978 1 78775 973 2
eISBN 978 1 78775 974 9

The Autism and Neurodiversity Self-Advocacy Handbook

Developing the Skills to Determine Your Own Future

Barb Cook
and Yenn Purkis

Jessica Kingsley Publishers
London and Philadelphia

First published in Great Britain in 2022 by Jessica Kingsley Publishers
An imprint of Hodder & Stoughton Ltd
An Hachette Company

1

A CIP catalogue record for this title is available from the
British Library and the Library of Congress

ISBN 978 1 78775 575 8
eISBN 978 1 78775 576 5

Printed and bound in Great Britain by TJ Books Limited

Jessica Kingsley Publishers' policy is to use papers that are natural,
renewable and recyclable products and made from wood grown in
sustainable forests. The logging and manufacturing processes are expected
to conform to the environmental regulations of the country of origin.

Jessica Kingsley Publishers
Carmelite House
50 Victoria Embankment
London EC4Y 0DZ

www.jkp.com

MIX
Paper from
responsible sources
FSC
www.fsc.org
FSC® C013056

Contents

Introduction

Neurodivergent people face many challenges in life. Being able to advocate for yourself is very useful and can help to avoid difficulties and address issues. However, not everyone has the skills or confidence to effectively self-advocate. This book aims to provide the skills and knowledge required to effectively advocate for yourself.

Drawing on the authors' extensive experience of advocacy – for themselves and the wider society – this book will give you the tools and strategies needed to advocate well. The book covers advocacy in many situations – at work, school and in your family and relationships. It also looks at ways of advocating in the wider community, such as through social media, presentation and writing. Advocacy skills make your life easier to navigate and help to build your confidence.

This book aims to provide you with the knowledge you need to advocate well and understand what actions may be helpful in different situations.

About the authors

Barb Cook

Barb received a diagnosis of Asperger syndrome (recently updated to Autism Level 1) along with attention deficit hyperactivity disorder (ADHD) combined type and phonological dyslexia in 2009 at the age of 40. This really did give the statement of 'life begins at 40' a whole lot more depth and meaning to Barb.

For Barb, it was literally a whole new beginning and set her life on a path of self-discovery, self-advocacy and personal empowerment.

Today, Barb is a developmental educator (DE) and autism and neurodiversity employment consultant for neurodivergent adults. As a developmental educator, Barb focuses on developing individualized learning strategies, tools and supports with positive outcomes for individuals across the lifespan. Barb is currently Deputy Chair of the Developmental Educators Australia Incorporated (DEAI), the governing body for developmental educators throughout Australia.

In 2016, Barb founded *Spectrum Women Magazine*. With nearly a million unique readers per year, the magazine is a place where autistic women and non-binary people from around the globe can write about their experiences and feel validated in reading about and recognizing themselves in others – a need that so many had been without for far too long. Barb is editor-in-chief of the magazine and it is one of her passions, as it provides trustworthy, relevant and credible information and a platform for fellow autistic people to have a voice.

Inspired by the magazine, Barb edited and co-authored *Spectrum Women: Walking to the Beat of Autism* with Dr Michelle Garnett, a clinical psychologist with over 20 years' experience of autism spectrum conditions. The book includes insights into life for women and non-binary

9

people on the autism spectrum, as 14 fellow autistics bare their hearts and souls, providing valuable information, validation, support and advice.

Barb is an independent autistic peer reviewer of the journal *Autism in Adulthood*, and she has completed a Master of Autism (Education) at the University of Wollongong (Australia) in the areas of education and employment. Barb was jointly awarded the 2018 Community Engagement Grant for facilitating the voice and self-determination of young adults on the autism spectrum and she is co-lead of this research project.

Barb is Vice Chair of the association My Life, My Decisions Inc. and Co-Design Committee Member of Aspergers Victoria's World of Work: Work Experience Pathways Project. She is on the Advisory Committee of Autism Awareness Australia's Autism: What Next? project and is a Community Council Member of AASET (Autistic Adults and other Stakeholders Engaged Together), which provides advice and input into the areas of research on autistic health. Through Barb's engagement with AASET, she has contributed to two published papers on autism and mental health in the academic publication *Autism*, by Sage Journals.

Barb is a committed autism advocate and writer, and a highly sought-after international speaker, making a variety of appearances on Australian radio, television, in newspapers and magazines and the short television documentary *The Chameleons: Women with Autism*.

In 2021, Barb was the winner of the A Different Brilliant Award at the Aspect National Recognition Awards for her work in autism advocacy, education and research, and recently received the Leadership Support Award for inclusive environment. She received a Special Commendation in the 2017 Autism Queensland Creative Futures Awards from the Queensland Governor, His Excellency Paul De Jersey.

Barb spoke at the World Autism Organization Congress 2018 in Houston, Texas, and was a keynote speaker for a special event, A Woman's Voice: Understanding Autistic Needs, for the National Institute of Mental Health in Washington DC in 2019.

Barb currently rides a Suzuki V-Strom DL1000 motorcycle called Ron 'Strom' Burgundy and he is one of the major loves of Barb's life. Her motorcycle keeps her anxiety levels in check by taking her out on adventurous rides around the countryside.

For more information on Barb and her extensive work, please visit www.barbcook.com.au.

Yenn Purkis

Yenn is an autistic and non-binary advocate who also has a diagnosis of schizophrenia. Yenn was diagnosed as autistic in 1994 but did not accept the diagnosis for a further seven years. Yenn was misdiagnosed with borderline personality disorder in 1996 and spent many years in and out of institutions because of this. What led Yenn to accepting their autism was some soul searching and reflection during an episode of mental illness. However, while Yenn accepted that they were indeed autistic, they did not really embrace the diagnosis until 2006 when their first book, an autobiography, was published.

Yenn became an autism advocate almost by default as a result of the publication of their first book. They began a journey of self-discovery and advocacy over the next few years. Yenn finally found their 'tribe' when they attended a seminar for autistic women and girls in 2009. Yenn's advocacy career took off a few years later when they met an autistic young man who was very disabled by the attitudes of others around his capability. Yenn was horrified when he called Yenn a liar when they said they were an autistic author and public servant. In the young man's view Yenn could not have career success as an autistic person. Yenn realized that they had to do something to ensure that an autism diagnosis was a positive and useful thing and not a reason to doubt people's capability.

After meeting this young man, Yenn's advocacy work went into overdrive. They wrote a book for autistic teens about preparing for employment. They were asked to audition for a TEDx talk and gave a talk on autism and resilience for TEDxCanberra in 2013. The book and the TEDx talk resulted in Yenn's profile as an advocate growing significantly larger.

Yenn now has a large profile on social media and is connected with a lot of individuals and organizations. Advocacy is Yenn's passionate interest and has been since 2012. Yenn has a number of awards for their advocacy work, including the 2016 ACT Volunteer of the Year and the 2019 ACT Chief Minister's Award for Achievement in Inclusion.

Yenn has facilitated a support group for autistic women and gender divergent folks in Canberra since 2011.

Yenn has spoken at dozens of events and conferences and has been featured in many media interviews including for SBS TV in 2019 news and as part of the 2010 documentary *Alone in a Crowded Room*.

Yenn is a member of the ACT Disability Justice Strategy Reference Group and the Aspect LGBTQ Steering Committee. They have no intention of changing their passionate interesting advocacy anytime soon! Yenn is sought after for their views on autism and has a nuanced and extensive knowledge of autism and related issues.

CHAPTER 1

What is Advocacy and Why Do We Need It?

What does neurodivergent mean?

The term neurodivergent refers to people who have one or more of a number of conditions, including – but not limited to – autism, dyslexia, attention deficit hyperactivity disorder (ADHD), attention deficit disorder (ADD), pathological demand avoidance (PDA), dyspraxia and Tourette's syndrome. In recent years, there has been a flourishing of the neurodiversity movement which aims to empower neurodivergent people and address ableism and discrimination. People who are not neurodivergent are known as neurotypical or allistic. These terms are not derogatory but are simply descriptive of people who are not neurodivergent. Allistic/neurotypical people can be effective allies in the neurodiversity movement.

What is neurodiversity?

Neurodiversity encompasses the many variations of the human brain, including what is considered the typical way of thinking. Neurodiversity embraces the fact that brain differences are not abnormal, but quite simply the many variations in the human brain – for example, autistic, dyslexic, ADHD – in how we think and perceive the world.

This concept of neurodiversity assists in reducing stigma around thinking, perceiving and learning differences we all have and encourages a more inclusive approach in valuing all minds and their differences, rather than pigeon-holing many people who differ from the assumed typical way of thinking and learning.

A good understanding of neurodiversity is valuable in education and employment – two highly important and significant aspects of our lives. Teachers and employers should be encouraged to take a step back and consider how they can change and adapt their current teaching methods or employment expectations to be inclusive for all people.

The situation for neurodivergent people today

While neurodivergent people are more empowered now in more ways than they have been in the past, there is still extensive discrimination and stigma. Neurodivergent people of all age groups face prejudice. Neurodiverse conditions are generally viewed as disabilities, and neurodivergent people face the broader range of discrimination others with disability face. This includes the following areas:

- Accessibility issues. This relates to accessing things like buildings, IT systems and parking. Many workplaces, education settings and retailers are inaccessible to people for a variety of reasons. Part of disability advocacy involves addressing accessibility issues. Access issues for neurodivergent people often centre around sensory accessibility.
- Ableism. This refers to discrimination against a person based on disability. Think racism, but for people with disability. Ableism can be overt (insults, discrimination in services etc.) or can be more subtle. Disabled people can also have internalized ableism where they are ableist against themselves.
- Domestic and family violence. People with disability face a greater rate of domestic and family violence than the general population. It can also be difficult for people with disability to access support and interventions to leave violent relationships. Abusers can deny their partner access to mobility or communication aids and can dismiss their partner's difficulties, leaving them doubting their own experience and thinking that they imagined the abuse.
- Access to employment. People with disability face discrimination

in employment, including recruitment processes like interviews. They can also face discrimination when they join the workforce. Attitudes of managers and colleagues can be problematic, or workplace premises may be inaccessible.

- Access to education. Education – school and tertiary – can involve discrimination for people with disability for a range of reasons.
- 'Inspiration porn'. This is the portrayal of people with disabilities as inspirational solely or in part on the basis of their disability. The term was coined in 2012 by the late disability rights activist Stella Young. Many people with disability who have a public profile are viewed through the lens of inspiration porn.
- Discrimination/exclusion in legal settings. People with disability can face difficulties in accessing legal services and can be discriminated against in criminal justice settings.

There are also some issues around discrimination that are more specific to neurodivergent people. These include:

- Sensory accessibility. Inclusive physical access to a building is essential but sensory access is also necessary. Things like fluorescent lights, odours from perfumes, and background noise can make it impossible for people to use a building. This can occur in workplaces and education settings as well as buildings used for leisure purposes, and homes.
- Conversion-type therapies for autistic people. Therapies like applied behaviour analysis (ABA) are highly problematic and operate on similar principles to gay conversion therapies by punishing autistic people – usually children – for doing things which come naturally for them, like stimming. The message these 'therapies' send is that it is not okay to be autistic. These 'therapies' represent significant discrimination against autistic people and are based in ableism.
- Autism cures. There are many charlatans who peddle 'cures' for autism. These generally have no therapeutic value and can be very dangerous (some charlatans market bleach enemas as a cure for autism, putting autistic children at risk). Neurodivergent people do not need a cure, even if there were an

effective one. They are wired differently rather than incorrectly, and the world benefits from having neurodivergent people. 'Cures' play on the fears of parents and are more about making money from anxious people than supporting anyone.

- Bullying. This is obviously not exclusive to neurodivergent people, but it is widespread, particularly in schools and in some workplaces. Neurodivergent people themselves can also be blamed for the bullying directed against them (think of the statement by a teacher, 'Your child wouldn't be bullied if they were more resilient'). Bullying is always the responsibility of the bully. Bullying can cause mental health issues and significant trauma for the victims.

- Forced eye contact. Eye contact is often seen as the pinnacle of communication even though it isn't. It is more a matter of retraining neurotypical people that not everyone needs to use eye contact in order to communicate, rather than forcing others to make eye contact.

- Prejudice in medical/health settings. Once again, this is not exclusive to neurodivergent people, but we get it a lot. Misdiagnoses of mental health conditions is very common. Some neurodivergent people will be so anxious about discrimination when accessing medical help that they simply refuse to access help. This is potentially very dangerous and is often the result of repeated invalidating experiences in health settings. Health clinicians need to understand neurodivergence better and to listen to neurodivergent people rather than making assumptions and working from stereotypes.

- Restraint (physical or chemical). There are periodically news items about a child being restrained at school which rightfully prompt horror in response. Neurodivergent people are also restrained by medications on occasion, which is less dramatic but equally wrong. Restraint comes from a view that we are violent or uncontrollable. If a neurodivergent person is violent it tends to be due to overload/meltdown or frustration around having no means of communication. Learning some de-escalation strategies or being given a communication device or augmented and alternative communication (AAC) tool are ways of addressing this without the need to use restraint. Building understanding of neurodivergence and behaviour for teachers and carers is a far better approach than restraining vulnerable people.

- Dismissal/gaslighting. Once again, this is not exclusive to neurodivergent people, but it happens a lot for us. Gaslighting is where a person dismisses your experience in order to make you question your sanity. It is a form of abuse. For neurodivergent people it doesn't always happen with an abusive partner. It can also be used by medical professionals and even employers. Because autistic people in particular tend to take things literally and honestly, it can be a very harmful experience as we assume those gaslighting us are correct and we must be mad.

Thankfully, there is a counter to these experiences. There are currently hundreds of neurodiversity advocates in the world who are fighting against these forms of discrimination. Advocacy is all about supporting people to be empowered and proud of who they are, as they are. Advocacy and activism are ways to address these forms of discrimination. Advocacy is global, and different advocates have different areas of interest.

Specific issues of intersectional groups

Intersectionality is a concept explaining disadvantage and diversity. People facing disadvantage include women, people with disability, people of colour (PoC), trans and gender diverse people, poor people, gay, lesbian, bi, pansexual and asexual people, people from culturally and linguistically diverse backgrounds, First Nations peoples, people who have a history of criminal justice system involvement, as well as many other groups.

In contrast to disadvantaged groups, there are groups of people with privilege. Privileged groups include cisgender men, heterosexual people, white people, non-disabled people and people with high socio-economic status.

Belonging to one of the disadvantaged groups results in social disadvantage but belonging to more than one group results in what is known as intersectional disadvantage. Disadvantage does not mean a person is going to have a dreadful life; and being privileged doesn't mean you are going to have a good life. The nature of intersectionality is about facing barriers to social participation rather than trying to predict what someone's life will be like.

The more intersectional groups are added, the harder it is likely to be for that person to achieve their goals. A person who is entirely privileged will not face any societal barriers to education, employment, healthcare and so on. It is important to note that individuals in these groups can be disadvantaged by circumstance, but they do not face societal barriers to success. For example, a white, cisgender heterosexual able-bodied man might fail their courses at university because they were not competent at their course rather than due to any weight of societal pressure on them.

Intersectionality is an important lens through which to understand barriers faced by neurodivergent people. Advocacy – and not just around neurodiversity – is a key way to address the disadvantage many people face. Working to address the societal barriers people face as a result of intersectional disadvantage is a better way to address disadvantage than assuming the person is struggling due to individual factors alone (such as incompetence at a course or inability to perform a work task). It is also important to understand that each element of disadvantage can be a part of a person's identity. A person may have a strong connection with one or other element of their identity.

So, what do we mean by 'advocacy'?

What is advocacy?

Advocacy is about helping someone to be heard and included in the decisions that affect their life. Advocacy aims to increase a person's control over their life and to develop a sense of empowerment and of being valued. Advocacy focuses on the needs and rights of that person. The word advocacy means 'to stand beside'. Advocacy involves standing beside someone and supporting them, even if that person is you. Advocacy is about promoting a person's rights and dignity. It is about change, challenging what is unfair, unjust or wrong.

This book focuses on self-advocacy. Self-advocacy is about speaking up for yourself and advocating to have your needs and rights met.

Self-advocates can enlist the help of allies or other advocates to convey their message.

What is self-advocacy and why do we need it?

Basically, self-advocacy is speaking up to get what you want. Everyone does this. It is making sure that your wishes and needs are made clear to another person and ensure that you have the same chances in life, the same rights and the opportunity to make the same choices as everyone else. Self-advocacy is a way to convey your thoughts and feelings. It also means being able to ask for help when you need it and being willing to ask for clarification, ask questions and learn new skills.

Knowledge is the key to self-advocacy. Like anything else, the more you know, the better you understand, and the easier it is to explain.

Self-determination

Self-determination means deciding what you want and making your own choices, and ensuring that you are involved in decision-making and have control of your life. Self-advocacy will help you convey what you want and to request that you be involved in all decisions that affect you. Self-advocacy is *not* giving the other person the answers they want to hear.

We self-advocate when we ask for support. This can be a request for more clarification on a task or assignment we need to do or conveying to the waiter in the restaurant that we are vegetarian or have certain food allergies. We certainly would not just eat food given to us if it were detrimental to our health or went against our personal values and morals. Food is a good example of where we will often speak up without questioning ourselves, as we know what we want.

So, we do have to ask ourselves, why in other situations do we stay quiet or feel afraid to ask for support, to ask for what we want, or to speak up or say no to something that we do not want to do or feel is wrong?

This book will explore how you can better determine what you want and how you can effectively speak up, speak out and self-advocate for what you want or need.

When do we learn to self-advocate and what does it achieve?

Ideally, these skills need to be taught and learned as soon as possible. Parents and teachers need to teach children how to advocate for themselves. Often with neurodivergent children, parents will advocate on their behalf for their needs and supports. Essentially, this is a good thing, but the individual also needs to be included in all decisions, which will assist in teaching them the skills to successfully advocate for themselves. Parents and educators can model self-advocacy skills to children and encourage them to ask for assistance without the fear of being judged or that they are doing it wrong.

Self-determination skills allow the person to discern what they do or do not want, identify their personal strengths and weaknesses, and be able to determine what they need to succeed – and communicate this to other people. When we understand what our specific needs are, which is often recognized through self-awareness, we can then formulate what we want and convey to other people what we need, and what our personal preferences and choices are.

So, for example, in a school setting, a student struggling with handwriting may find it difficult to take a lot of handwritten notes, or quickly write down personal notes that they need to help them learn, do their homework, or complete an assignment. Without some kind of support, this student is going to find it difficult to keep up and be able to write down useful notes that they can refer to later to assist them with learning or completing a task.

When the student has good self-determination skills, they will realize that taking notes in class is a challenge for them. Now, what they can do is to self-advocate and ask the lecturer or the teacher if they can use a recording device that they can refer to at a later time instead of taking written notes.

Accommodating teachers or lecturers will say yes to this request. But if the student is declined their support needs, they then need to have good self-advocacy skills to address this situation and to discuss what other options can be considered, or if their request for support is still declined, to take it further in having their support needs met. For example, they may want to speak with the department coordinator or the disability services department and explain to them that they need these supports to help them to best succeed in their educational journey and they are crucial to their learning.

Learning about ourselves

When we struggle with having good self-advocacy and self-determination skills, we often find that we can struggle in nearly all aspects of our lives. This can lead to significant anxiety for neurodivergent people and potentially, in the long term, to depression, due to not having their needs and supports met.

As previously mentioned, parents can be great advocates for their children, but also need to teach them the skills to be able to advocate for themselves. When a child is taught how to self-advocate and determine what their needs are, it allows them to learn to identify their challenges, and how to find solutions or work out what best supports them, which the parents or educators may not know or realize due to neurological differences, and ways of learning and understanding the world around them.

However, even though external support is great, we often know ourselves best. When we are taught and encouraged to self-advocate, it also builds self-confidence and self-esteem, and in turn, will help us to learn more about how we can help ourselves. This self-confidence also creates a sense of ownership of our lives, and this learning about ourselves is working towards a sense of independence and empowerment.

When we learn these skills, especially at a younger age, it will make a significant impact in the long run. It reduces our sense of feeling powerless, and that we need to depend on other people to help us, especially in conveying what we need. When neurodivergent people learn these skills, and use them, for example in educational and employment settings, it can encourage them to ask their peers and work colleagues for help or feel confident to explain to them why they need extra or different support.

When we feel empowered in being able to advocate for ourselves, the feelings of fear and anxiety are reduced, allowing us to speak freely about concerns, which in turn, builds on our self-confidence and value.

How do we self-advocate and know what works for us?

We need to be able to identify early in life, where possible, that we may be struggling with doing, say, a task, a particular way. If we have never been allowed to explore or look at different ways that can help us in our learning or working environment, how do we know what supports to ask for?

This is where educators, parents and employers can also help neurodivergent people improve their self-advocacy and self-determination skills, by giving them regular feedback in a positive manner. This can be done by identifying first what their strengths are, and then highlighting where they have observed that the neurodivergent person may need some support.

Now on the flip side, a neurodivergent person may see something at school, at university, or in the workplace that could be done differently and that may benefit not just them but the whole environment and everyone in that environment.

When we work collaboratively together, through actively listening and acting, we are working towards a far more inclusive environment. When neurodivergent people are encouraged that asking for help and speaking up is a good thing, they are encouraged to self-advocate for themselves.

Person-centred approach

By having open conversations about different learning and thinking styles and stressing that a neurological difference is not a deficit, just a difference, young people can be show pathways to actively and freely speak up for themselves. And this needs to be encouraged in all aspects of their lives.

Again, when the neurodivergent person is younger, they must be helped to determine and self-advocate for what support they need in the classroom. The young person also needs to be included where possible in all decisions about their support needs, goals and vision setting.

For example, a student may have an individualized education plan (IEP) in place that has been determined and created by health professionals, educators and parents, with the anticipation that the student was involved in the discussion about what supports they may require. When this IEP is implemented in the educational setting, it also must encourage the student to be actively part of understanding what their supports and needs are, and how to ask for these. Also, they should be taught how to recognize when they may require a support in an upcoming situation.

When students are allowed to actively think freely about what will help them, this encourages good self-advocacy and self-determination skills. At times, their ideas and decisions may need some guidance, especially if they feel a particular support may be helpful, when in reality it may be detrimental to their learning or well-being. Parents and educators need to be able to productively communicate with them about the potential outcomes of their choices and help them find more positive and healthier solutions for themselves. Again, this must be in consultation with the neurodivergent individual at every stage, not making the changes for them without their consent, and giving clear and constructive reasons why their decision may not be the best choice for them.

Taking the active and positive support approach while the neurodivergent person builds their self-advocacy and self-determination skills will empower them with life-long skills for all aspects of their lives and give them a sense of ownership in all decisions and choices they make.

Neurodivergent people always need the opportunity to learn and to identify what will support them in a positive or constructive way. They need to be allowed at all ages and stages of life to try and identify the cause of the situation and to find a solution, before parents, educators, employers or friends step in and provide a solution for them. When they are given this opportunity to think for themselves first, they are reducing their need to rely on others to do the advocating, thinking and problem-solving for them. But also, if the individual asks for support in helping them find a solution, stakeholders must be willing to offer advice that explains why a person should consider a particular suggestion. Information is the key to helping them consider other options.

Learning about legal rights as an advocate

It is vital as a self-advocate to be aware of your legal rights and the legal rights afforded to all neurodiverse people. This will help you to ensure you are working within the law and most importantly to understand your rights and the rights of those working with you. This section covers your rights as an advocate under the law within Australia.

Know your legal rights – education

Another thing neurodivergent people of all ages need to learn is what their legal rights are and how to talk about them in a constructive and positive way. These legal rights can include things such as their rights to a fair and equal education. This can mean that a person who has a disability is entitled to the same opportunity and choices in education as students without a disability. For example, in Australia, all educational providers – this means preschool, primary school, high school, vocational education, university and independent educational institutions – have an obligation to their students with a disability, or those with additional support and learning needs, to ensure they have equal opportunities as all the other students in education. This is reinforced under the Disability Standards. It is enacted in law under the Disability Discrimination Act 1992 in Australia. Many countries have similar legislative instruments to protect the rights of people with disability.

However, this does not mean that every student will have the exact same experience. What the legislation means is that students with a disability should have the same opportunities and choices in education as those students without a disability. This can be done through making reasonable adjustments in the classroom, to the environment or to the learning programme or curriculum that is being delivered. For a class to be truly inclusive, educators need to make reasonable adjustments to the content they are delivering, to allow all students to learn to their best ability, and to allow the students who need supports to be able to ask for them.

Legal rights in education also cover...

In the education and training setting, the educational standards cover more than just the classroom environment and learning. They also cover enrolment, participation, curriculum development, accreditation and delivery, student support services, and the elimination of harassment and victimization.

The key aspects of the standards also require schools and training and education providers to treat students with a disability on the same basis as students without disability, to make reasonable adjustments to students' learning programmes and learning environment, and to consult with the student or their parents or caregivers or support workers on the reasonable adjustments that will be provided.

Disability Discrimination Act (Australia) in employment

The Disability Discrimination Act (Australia) protects people in many areas of public life. Apart from education, this Act is applicable in employment, in regards to getting a job, what the conditions and terms are of a job, training for a job and training within a job, promotions or moving up the ladder at work, and also in conflict resolution, mediation and how dismissals are handled. There are similar acts in the USA, UK and a number of other countries.

Disability Discrimination Act in public life

This Act also protects people when they rent or buy a house or a unit, and when they visit public areas such as parks, government offices, restaurants, hotels or shopping centres. It also protects a person when they are using or getting a service. This includes things like banking, insurance, or services provided by government departments, like the National Disability Insurance Scheme (NDIS) in Australia, welfare payments and child support. It also covers things like public transport and services that are provided by doctors or therapists. It is also relevant for trained staff providing services in places like restaurants and retail shopping and entertainment venues.

The Act can protect people from harassment because of a disability; for example, being discriminated against because of their neurological difference or learning needs.

Empowering yourself by knowing your rights

When we educate and arm ourselves with the knowledge of our rights, and learn where we are being discriminated against, we are effectively empowering ourselves to actively enforce our rights when we are in situations that are discriminating against us. These discriminating situations are disempowering us and dehumanizing us, and this is where having good self-advocacy and self-determination skills will help to identify when this is happening and allow us to speak up and put a stop to it, or if it doesn't stop, we can then take further action. When we are afraid to speak up or do not know our rights, we can become trapped in situations that are detrimental to our mental well-being and our self-esteem.

Fear of taking action

In situations that require action due to discrimination, it can be quite difficult and anxiety-provoking. When we have come from a background where we have felt disempowered through previous job losses, for example, often not due to our fault or our capability to work but to being discriminated against at work, we feel incredibly anxious about speaking up or asking for support.

Often this discrimination comes from lack of knowledge of people with neurological differences. Work colleagues or supervisors may view the neurodivergent person as difficult or lazy when they do not fit in with the workplace or keep up with the demands. When workplaces do not listen or actively support people who require support to do their job effectively, or allow a neurodivergent employee to implement their own supports that will enable them to perform the job better, these workplaces are discriminating against these people by not supporting them and making assumptions about their work performance, rather than communicating with them and encouraging them to do what is best for themselves.

When a neurodivergent person has experienced this type of discrimination over many years, they feel afraid to self-advocate and determine if they should speak up and ask for support when they are rightly entitled to it, so will often stay quiet and struggle in silence.

When someone has been subjected to feeling like a failure because of the difference in how they perform and think, they may despair of ever having a happy working future.

Not being understood or heard

How can we gain good self-advocacy and self-determination skills, especially if we have not been taught the skills early on in life, or have been subjected to negative experiences over a long period of time? Young neurodivergent people, especially those who are transitioning from school and out into the workforce, often have high levels of anxiety and fear about what lies ahead for them. Research has identified that this is due to not being able to identify what they want to do with their future or having the opportunity to successfully communicate to educators and parents what they want for their future.

Many young neurodivergent people feel their thoughts, goals, visions and dreams for the future are being dismissed or just not being heard. These young adults feel unable to communicate what they would like for the future, and as if no one truly understands them.

Many feel as though they are being shaped to fit into a society that is not designed for them and how they think. They can often feel like an outsider, having to ask for help, or being disregarded or viewed as difficult. Without having someone who truly understands them and helps to support and encourage them to actively speak up and self-advocate, they can become withdrawn, highly anxious and depressed.

Therefore, for neurodivergent people, being in an environment, such as that provided by tailored in-person training and workshops, that understands them and accepts them can make them feel safe and encourage them to freely express themselves. These environments are often where neurologically like-minded people come together, no longer feeling as though they are the alien or the outsider but actually part of a group where people 'get' them. Essentially it is a bit like finding their tribe. They will often come out of their shell, sharing their experiences with fellow people in the group, and gain a sense of validation and understanding that their way of thinking and perceiving is not defective but just different.

Case study: Ellie

Ellie is nine years old, autistic and has ADHD. She received her autism diagnosis at the age of five and ADHD at seven. When Ellie started primary school, she had no friends and was ostracized and bullied by the other kids. This took a huge toll on her sense of self-esteem and identity. Ellie didn't tell her parents that she was being bullied and that she felt very alone at school. When she was eight, Ellie made friends with another autistic child who had recently started at her school. This made all the difference and Ellie was much happier. Her parents noticed the difference in her, even though they had been unaware of the bullying issues. Ellie told her parents how she felt much happier with her new friend and how the other kids were less mean to her. This knowledge helped her parents to support her and have conversations about how she was doing at school.

Situations in which neurodivergent people can feel safe to speak freely also provide an opportunity to discuss what will help them self-advocate and self-determine, without feeling anxious or self-conscious.

Preparing for advocacy: identifying your strengths and weaknesses

Gaining back your power

As previously identified, recognizing what our strengths and weaknesses are will help us in self-advocating and determining for ourselves what we need in terms of support. Knowing our strengths and weaknesses is also key to knowing what our goals and visions are for the future. When we don't know what these are or are how to ask for support in learning what opportunities there are for us, it will inevitably lead to us not knowing what we want to do or where to start.

Identifying strengths and weaknesses, along with goal setting and vision planning, should start as young as possible but is not limited to any age. You can do this at any stage of your life. It is also good in helping you to re-evaluate if what you are currently doing is serving you, or if you need to change what you are doing to make yourself happier.

When you realize that it is never too late to make a change to your life that is determined by you, it can be incredibly empowering. When you speak up for what you want or speak out when you are not happy with the situation you are in, you are taking back your power and learning to self-advocate positively and productively, determining that you need to make these changes for yourself, rather than staying quiet and stuck in situations that are disempowering or demoralizing to you.

Making these decisions and learning to change your thinking and embracing the fact that you do have value and worth also means you do not have to do this alone. If you have been subjected to long-term negative environments or have been diagnosed in mid or late life, you will most likely need support through mentors with the same neurology, as well as professional support to help you deal with the anxiety, depression and low self-esteem that often come from being exposed to recurrent negative situations.

It is through collaborative support that you can be helped with your sense of self and worth and to understand that your voice needs to be heard, listened to and acted on when deciding and advocating for your needs and supports.

Case study: Riley

Riley is a kind and intelligent person with ADHD. Riley was bullied throughout their school career. They were given very negative messaging about themselves and after such a long time being given this messaging they took it on board and thought that the hateful words and accusations were true. Riley thought, *Why would so many people say those things if they weren't true?* The bullies told Riley that they were stupid and weird. Riley took this with them into their adult life and avoided situations requiring sensitivity and intelligence as they thought they were incapable of these sorts of things. When Riley was 30, they had an appointment with a psychiatrist. The psychiatrist took Riley's history and as they were leaving commented that Riley was clearly very intelligent. Riley was amazed and denied that they were intelligent. The doctor gave examples from Riley's story that demonstrated Riley's clear intellect. It was the first time in their life that anyone had called Riley intelligent. Riley asked some of their friends what they thought about the idea of Riley being intelligent and they all responded positively. Riley started to see themselves differently and to challenge the negative messaging they had been given by bullies and which they had taken on board in the absence of any conflicting evidence.

Goal setting and vision planning

Understanding our strengths and weaknesses helps us to determine what we would like our goals, visions and dreams to be. Goal setting is key in building self-advocacy. When we learn who we are, we can determine what we want. So, ascertaining what direction you would like your future to take requires some careful consideration and time to reflect on what you want, not on what other people expect. Again, this can be done at any age.

When we are younger and still at school, we learn, with the help of parents and teachers, to identify what we really like doing and how using our interests and strengths can help determine what future we would like to have. This is also applicable when we are older and re-evaluating where our life currently is, whether we are still enjoying what we do, or if we're not enjoying what we're doing, to take a good look at what we can do to implement change.

For example, if you were diagnosed in later life, you may only now be realizing what your true strengths are; what has challenged you in the past will now become clear and you can learn how you can best support yourself. In the past, you may not have realized that you were experiencing, say, sensory overwhelm, due to your working environment making you stressed and anxious. You may have enjoyed doing the work but could never figure out why being at work made you feel mentally overwhelmed by the end of the day or the end of the week.

Once we start to learn about ourselves, our support needs and what will help us, we can then self-advocate to those around us, explaining that by having the right supports in place, we can perform better and reduce our personal overwhelm or anxiety.

So how do we go about goal setting? What we first need to do is identify what it is that we want to work towards. We also need to understand how long this goal could take, and whether short-term goals need to be set to assist in reaching long-term goals. Often, neurodivergent people will have an idea of their overall goal, so from this vision, the best way to understand how to achieve this is to work backwards from this large-scale goal.

In breaking down a long-term goal into smaller, more achievable goals, we also learn to identify what challenges we may have to overcome and where our strengths can help us with determining what supports, tools or strategies we may need to put in place to help us get to this long-term goal.

As previously discussed, when we learn to identify what our weaknesses and strengths are, it helps us in understanding ourselves better and gives us greater clarity on how to ask for support. When we do not have a clear picture of what we need support or assistance with, it can make it difficult to articulate exactly what we need and what this type of support may consist of.

Goal setting can be a very powerful process in helping to motivate us to turn our visions into reality. Ask yourself what you want to achieve once you reach that goal (for example, gaining that dream job). Is this long-term goal of working towards the job that you want also part of a bigger picture of earning a good income so that you can buy a nice car or a place of your own to live in? By planning and identifying these key points, you are not only improving and growing your self-advocacy and self-determination, but you also are working towards a more independent life.

Case study: Yenn

I was diagnosed as autistic in 1994 at the age of 20. I was in denial about my diagnosis for a further seven years, believing that autism equated to intellectual disability – something I had been bullied about as a child and teen. I was very troubled to think I was autistic, even if deep down I knew the diagnosis to be correct. Even when I came to accept my autism, I was still not very enthusiastic about it and was more comfortable telling people I had spent time in prison than that I was autistic.

I gradually came to terms with my autism, but it was meeting an autistic mentor which helped me to embrace it. I met Polly Samuel at a course for autistic public speakers. We immediately hit it off and became friends. Over the next few months, Polly became my autism world mentor. She encouraged me to write my life story. It took four weeks to draft, two weeks to edit and three weeks for the publisher to say yes to publishing it. Although she played a part in my first book coming into existence, even more significantly, Polly taught me about autistic pride. I would spend ages at her home looking at all her stimmy things, artwork and the trappings of her life as an advocate and autism world celebrity. I loved spending time with Polly. She was the first person who supported my advocacy career and taught me to be proud of my amazing autistic self. Thanks to Polly I am now a mentor and advocate myself – and a many times published author too! I am eternally grateful to Polly for her gift of mentorship.

Independence: it is not what you think

Independence is a word that is often loaded with meaning. In many situations, we often need help from other people to achieve our dreams and visions. For example, if you are buying a car, you need support and advice to ascertain if the car has been well maintained, so you could ask a mechanic to check it over for you before you buy it. You may do your research on what type of car you want to buy, but by also asking people who have had this type of car what it was like, you get a better insight into whether this type of car is for you, and if there have been any problems other people have experienced that have not been documented by the manufacturer.

As you can see, you are working independently in doing your homework, but you are also asking for advice and information from other people to help you in making your decision. If we do not do the research or ask other people, we may well end up buying a dodgy car, or have a car that could potentially have problems further on down the track.

It is the same in all other situations. We always need advice, support and information to help us determine if this product, this career choice or education is what we really want. So, with self-advocacy and self-determination, you will often find that your decisions are made in collaboration with other outside sources. These outside sources can help you make your decisions, but ultimately the decisions are yours, and determined by the information that has been presented to you.

Barriers you may experience

Disclosure

Disclosure of your differences and/or disability may or may not have an effect on gaining the supports you need. Disclosure is something that is personal and it is ultimately your choice alone as to whether you decide to disclose to your employer, your educator, your friends or family.

If you feel that by disclosing you will be held back and it will affect your opportunity to gain your support needs, then you are under no obligation to disclose what your diagnosis is. The only time you must disclose is if you are required by law or applying for a job where medical conditions must be disclosed. If the conditions are not disclosed during the application process, it could be viewed negatively and you could potentially lose your job if you are successful in gaining employment.

But if you require a variety of supports or feel that disclosing will be beneficial to gaining supports, it is certainly something to consider. For example, in educational settings such as university, if you disclose to the disability services department that you may need a longer time to complete assignments or exams, or that you experience sensory overwhelm, they must put in place reasonable measures to provide accommodations for you. This again comes under the Australian Disability Discrimination Act 1992 and similar legislative instruments in other countries, and if they do not provide reasonable supports, then they are in breach of this act.

When you decide to disclose, you need to consider whether you do this prior to starting a job, shortly after starting a job, or further down the track when experiencing challenges, and need supports put in place which can't be done without disclosure.

What you do need to be mindful of is that if you are experiencing difficulties and challenges at work and have not asked for help when you first started experiencing these challenges, it can be detrimental to your well-being and also the possibility of keeping the job. If you have been struggling long term without accommodations or supports, it can also have an effect on other work colleagues around you. If you're experiencing challenges that are extremely stressful and may lead you to being overwhelmed, or set off a meltdown in the workplace, this may be very concerning to your work colleagues.

When we find it overwhelmingly difficult to self-regulate our emotions, we may inadvertently lash out at a work colleague over something that generally is quite small and could be approached in a different way. When we are feeling calm, we are much less likely to react negatively or impulsively, and find it easier to control our emotions and how we are feeling. Outbursts, anger, frustration and meltdowns are a sign that a person is not coping or has been struggling far too long without support. Often it is not until this point is reached that action is taken in how to provide help. When we don't ask for support or ask for it early enough, these situations can occur, and often on a regular basis.

Disclosing early will help; for example, the employer may understand and try to accommodate your needs, and if you disclose to your work colleagues this will help them to identify if you appear to be overwhelmed or stressed at work. It will also encourage them to ask you if you're doing okay and if you need support. Working together is to your benefit, and to the benefit of the whole workplace. It creates an environment where it is safe to ask for help and support.

Case study: Yenn

I joined the Australian Public Service in 2007 as a graduate. I have worked in the service continuously since then and love my job, most of the time. I have been promoted twice and have received awards from the chief executive officers (CEOs) of two different departments. I have a high profile as an autistic and disability advocate in the Public Service and frequently give presentations on autism and disability to both my own and other departments.

I disclosed my autism in the first stage of the application process for my first role. I wasn't worried about the impact it might have on my chances, mainly due to naivety. It didn't occur to me that anyone would discriminate against me as I didn't see any reason for them to. I know that for others this might have been an error of judgement but in my case, there were no issues in my application. When I had the interview, the chair of the panel asked if there was anything they could do to support me during the interview. I couldn't think of anything, but she suggested maybe one of the panel should ask me all the questions rather than the usual practice of all panel members asking questions. This was a good reasonable adjustment and I found it helpful.

> I used to lend my managers a copy of my autobiography as I figured it would help them understand me as an autistic person. I haven't done that for several years now, but I do talk to my managers and colleagues about my experiences and perspective. I am mostly quite popular at work and people seem to think I am quirky and very honest. I have not had a lot of experience of bullying or discrimination at work although I know others who have disclosed disabilities and it has resulted in difficulties for them. I tend to think there is no right or wrong about disclosure. In some of my previous workplaces I have elected to not disclose and in others I have been out loud and proud. I always suggest that people have a strategy around whether they disclose and, if they do, at what stage in the employment process they should do it, what they should say, how much they should say and who they should say it to. In my own experience, disclosing at work has been almost entirely positive but there have also been some challenges around it and I can feel a bit exposed at times.

What is an ally?

An ally is an allistic/neurotypical person who genuinely supports the neurodiversity movement and neurodivergent people. A good ally will take a back seat to the people they are supporting and will not make the conversation all about them. A good ally supports people to self-advocate. An ally uses their position of privilege to learn from neurodivergent people and to support their cause. A genuine ally is a great support for neurodivergent people and can help with advocacy.

Resources

There are many advocacy resources for neurodivergent people. These include blogs written by other advocates, videos, books and webinars. Resources can be content created by neurodivergent people and sometimes by genuine allies as well. There are a number of advocacy websites and groups. Resources are available from around the world. Social media has a range of advocacy resources although it is important to be cautious with online groups on social media as some are less reputable than others. Neurodivergent-run groups are often best but there are some helpful ally groups too. You can start up an online page or group yourself. There is more information on this later in this book.

CHAPTER 2

Practical Steps to Advocacy

How to advocate

Advocacy can take many forms, such as:

- Having a positive attitude about being neurodivergent/embracing your identity.
- Speaking to people in positions of authority to convey a point and drive an outcome.
- Being involved in celebrating days of significance, such as Autistic Pride Day.
- Explaining neurodivergent perspectives.
- Meeting with other neurodivergent people.
- Giving presentations on neurodiversity at work/school.
- Engaging in civil/political life, promoting the needs of neurodivergent people.
- Being kind to yourself.
- Giving people helpful advice based on your lived experience.
- Supporting neurodivergent kids.
- Being active in social media groups.
- Engaging in creative output – art exhibitions, comedy and so on – about neurodiversity.
- Starting a social or support group for neurodivergent people.
- Challenging ableist views in conversations.
- Starting a group or becoming an administrator for a social media group focused on advocacy.
- Being interviewed for media.
- Publishing articles/blogs/books on neurodiversity.

There is no one right way to do advocacy. It can involve a range of activities. No one form of advocacy is 'better' than another. As long as the message is positive and helpful, that is the main thing. You do not need to spend all your time advocating and it does not need to be a big effort. With advocacy, every little helps so do what you can.

How do you develop advocacy skills?

Advocacy skills are not generally acquired overnight. They come about from practice and experience over time. The experiences we have feed into our level of knowledge and wisdom, culminating in the development of skills in advocacy. Sometimes difficult experiences can be fruitful in the development of advocacy skills. For example, being discriminated against may make someone angry and filled with a need to right the wrong, leading to the development of advocacy skills. However, at times positive experiences feed and bolster our advocacy capability. For example, having a family full of love and respect is likely to give a person skills and confidence to advocate for themselves when they need to.

It is possible to consciously build advocacy skills through viewing experiences in terms of possible advocacy opportunities. Almost every experience offers an opportunity to develop our skills. Advocacy has a variety of elements, including refuting damaging/discriminatory statements, promoting autistic/neurodivergent pride, supporting other neurodivergent people, employment advocacy, housing advocacy, education advocacy, supporting neurodivergent children and being a role model or mentor to others.

You can view almost every interaction and encounter as an opportunity to develop advocacy skills such as:

- representation
- defending yourself and others against attacks and ableism
- mentoring
- standing up for yourself
- activism
- education
- having a public profile as an advocate
- role modelling.

Case study: Dylan

Dylan is autistic and works in a corporate job. One of his co-workers who has ADHD was experiencing some difficult behaviour from their manager and confided in Dylan. Dylan had witnessed some of the poor behaviour from this manager and was upset by it. It made him feel uncomfortable and he wanted to support his co-worker. Dylan encouraged the co-worker to speak to the manager's manager and also put them in touch with the workplace employee assistance programme for free counselling. The co-worker thanked Dylan and said they were a great advocate. The problematic manager was moved to a different area and the co-worker was much happier. Dylan had never seen himself as an advocate before but was really happy to assist his co-worker and was glad his advice had been helpful.

Representation

Representation is all about working on promoting positive representation of neurodivergent people in things like news media and the online world. It is an important area of advocacy and often gets addressed by organizations such as the Autistic Self Advocacy Network (ASAN) and individual activists. How neurodivergent people are represented in media is a really important area as it largely determines how people view our community.

Defending others

Defending others is an important part of advocacy. It can be done in a variety of forums. It may involve a parent supporting their child at school or calling out a bully or troll online. Sometimes it is easier to defend someone else than to stand up for yourself.

Mentoring

Mentoring is about sharing knowledge, skills and life experience to guide another towards reaching their potential. Having a mentor can be really helpful for people wanting to be advocates. Being a mentor is also an important part of advocacy for many neurodivergent people. It is possible to both be a mentor and have a mentor.

Another critical support that has been found to be incredibly useful for neurodivergent people is having a mentor who has the same neurology as them. Also, it is good to have a mentor who has had life experiences in the areas where you are seeking support. Having a mentor you can talk to who will not judge you but can offer personal insights and experiences and explain how they overcame the challenges, for example at school or in the workplace, can provide unique and valuable information that you can implement in your daily life.

Another reason why mentoring is incredibly important, especially for young adults, is that once a neurodivergent person leaves school, support and services are significantly reduced. If they haven't had good self-advocacy or self-determination skills taught to them, then how are they able to determine their future and life ahead of them?

When an individual hasn't had the opportunity to identify what their goals and visions are for the future or been able to act on and work towards these, they are limited in their ability to determine and work towards their future, their way.

Considerations when choosing a mentor

Some of the main things to look for when you are considering a mentor are:

- Does the mentor have the same neurology as you?
- What experience does the mentor have in the areas that you are seeking support for?
- Can the mentor provide testimonials of previous clients?

Where do you find a mentor?

A mentor is a good thing to have but where do you find one? There are many ways to connect with a mentor:

- Through the online autism community.
- In social groups – friends can become mentors sometimes. In fact, a mentoring relationship can be seen as a sort of friendship with a positive power dynamic. It is important to note that there is a difference between a friendship and a mentoring relationship.
- In the workplace or an education setting. Yenn found their mentor Polly Samuel at a training course for autistic adults.
- Through a neurodivergent-led organization. In Australia, the I CAN Network provides mentoring support for autistic school kids and young adults. The organization employs dozens of autistic people as mentors and supports their development.
- Through other organizations – for example, lesbian, gay, bisexual, transgender, queer or questioning, intersex and asexual (LGBTQIA+) organizations. Neurodivergent people often belong to other diversity groups. Being neurodivergent is often not our only identity, This can mean we prefer to have a mentor from a different diversity group, or who shares our particular combination of intersectional groups.

What a mentor does and does not do

Mentors can do many things. They can:

- provide you with tools, strategies and insights
- give advice and support
- be someone you can confide in about difficult experiences
- be someone you can share triumphs and successes with
- be a leader or support you to take on your own leadership role
- provide advice and insights about your advocacy and other elements of what you do
- be a sounding board for your ideas
- be a venting buddy – but be aware that while there is a place for venting, it is not actually taking action and alone venting cannot address issues
- support you to raise issues and concerns
- challenge you in a respectful way.

We also need to be aware of what a mentor is not. A mentor:

- is not a mental health therapist
- should not be controlling
- should not be discriminatory, ableist or paternalistic
- should never harass or bully you
- cannot provide assessments or medical advice
- is not your manager or supervisor
- is not there to be your friend.

What services a mentor may provide

Some of the key tasks of a mentor may include:

- Getting to know the client and letting the client get to know them.
- Listening to the client and discussing anything that is worrying them.
- Valuing their opinions and beliefs.
- Encouraging them to achieve their objectives.
- Talking about relevant experiences/problems they have over-come (if appropriate).
- Encouraging clients to talk and think about their ambitions and hopes for the future and plan the steps needed to get there.

In particular, a mentor will work towards achieving positive change at a time of transition, through goal setting and motivation.

Case study: Elise

Elise is 16 and dyslexic. She had been struggling with confidence and felt very embarrassed a lot of the time. She had always found school chal-lenging but as she got older her anxiety increased and this contributed to her lack of confidence in herself. Elise's mum thought she might benefit from having a mentor or role model who was also dyslexic. Elise's mum attended a conference on dyslexia and met one of the speakers, Hannah, who is dyslexic and runs her own neurodiversity consultancy business. After talking with Elise's mum, Hannah agreed to connect with Elise. At first, Elise was uncomfortable about the idea of talking with Hannah but this changed pretty much as soon as they met. Hannah and Elise got along really well together and have a lot in common. Knowing Hannah has been an excellent experience for Elise and her confidence has grown and her social anxiety has decreased. Elise is even doing better at school due to her increased confidence and she has made some new friends around her own age too. Elise loves having Hannah as a mentor and says, 'She gets it. I can talk to her about things I am going through and she understands it. She is an awesome person.'

Standing up for yourself

This is probably what people think of when you say advocacy, but it can be harder than other forms of advocacy. It can take practice to build your confidence in order to advocate for yourself. It can also help to have others support you as you advocate for yourself. Even people who have been advocates for some time can struggle to stand up for themselves, so it can help to start small, such as calling out someone you know and trust.

Activism

Activism is closely related to advocacy and there is a lot of overlap between both activities. Activism is more about calling people or organizations out that are doing negative things or being discriminatory. Activism is often done by organizations so if you want to do some activism it can help to get in contact with them.

Education

Sadly, the world is full of ignorant people. Education is an element of advocacy which can be quite fraught, with many people rightfully saying that it should not be the job of neurodivergent people to educate ignorant people. This makes for a challenging area, as education is in fact necessary. You will need to decide whether you want to participate in this area. Educating people can be very frustrating but can have some good outcomes. With educating others, it can help to set boundaries for yourself around how much education you want to do, which people in your life you are comfortable with educating and what areas you want to educate in.

Having a public profile

Some neurodiversity advocates have a public profile. Both authors of this book fit that category. There are literally hundreds of other neurodivergent people with public profiles – with books, a social media presence, presentations and so on – but this is definitely not the only way to be an advocate. In fact, there are many, many more people doing advocacy than there are 'public' neurodiversity advocates.

Case study: Vinh

Vinh is autistic and a very talented visual artist. He has always been quite shy and introverted and never saw himself as an advocate. One of Vinh's friends, Seb, who is also autistic, asked Vinh to collaborate on a graphic novel. Vinh thought this was a wonderful idea and did the illustrations for the novel while Seb wrote the text. Vinh was happy to illustrate the novel but never thought it would result in any publicity or opportunities for advocacy. Vinh was very surprised when the book was published and even more so when it attracted media attention.

Vinh found it difficult to participate in media interviews but he was always with Seb when they had to do media, which helped. Vinh also found he had an unexpected profile in the autism community. While it was quite anxiety-provoking, over time Vinh got used to being sought out for his opinions. His confidence grew and he actually started putting himself forward for media and other public-facing advocacy activities, not because he wanted to be 'famous' but because he wanted to share his experiences and what he had learned in life with other people, and help them navigate the world well.

Role models

Role models are similar to mentors. The main difference is that role models can be more distant than mentors. A role model is someone you admire and look up to and whose work you learn from. A mentor tends to be a bit more hands on. You tend to have a conscious relationship with a mentor whereas a role model can be someone you have never met but whose work you admire. Many advocates have role models. A role model can help you on your advocacy journey.

How to communicate and resolve conflict as an advocate

Communication

There are sometimes situations where mediation between the employee and employer is necessary due to communication breakdown. Often this is not until it's too late and employee well-being is at crisis point and the employer is at a loss as to how to resolve the situation. There is a stalemate between what the employer expects of the employee and the employee's expectation of what the employer should be doing for them.

In these situations, emotions can run extremely high due to the employee feeling as though they are failing or as though the workplace has failed them. This causes immense tensions between the employee and the employer that lead to situations where third parties are contacted as a last resort in a desperate need to find a solution.

When things are left too long, it often takes a significant number of support strategies and resources to help the employee feel comfortable in returning to work and that they will be listened to and genuinely supported. From the employer's perspective, they will feel that they need to ensure that the employee is able to do their duties to the expectations of the employer and that the well-being of the whole workplace is taken into consideration.

The employee may also be feeling self-conscious and anxious in returning to work out of fear of what may have been disclosed, or what is being perceived by work colleagues while they have been away from work, especially if it has been long term.

As you can see, not having good self-advocacy skills and/or a good insight into oneself can lead to challenging situations further down the track. When we know what our strengths and weaknesses are, what we find challenging and what we find we do well at, this encourages us to feel less anxious and openly ask for support earlier.

Good employers will welcome employees who are upfront and open about difficulties they may be experiencing in the workplace. When good and open communication is initiated and embraced this works towards ensuring that the employee and the whole workplace are being supported in the best way possible.

Conflict

Another area that needs strong self-advocacy skills is when we experience conflict.

Conflict is inevitable when a number of people work together. Conflict can be described as a difference in opinion or some kind of disagreement between two or more people. Conflicts need to be resolved effectively. It is important not only to resolve the conflict, but also to ensure that everyone involved in the conflict does not unnecessarily end up being in any kind of emotional stress during the resolution process. Finding a balance between resolving the conflict and maintaining the emotional well-being of people involved is critical to a successful outcome.

Hence it is important to understand clearly what a conflict is, why it occurs, what the challenges are in resolving the conflict and what various resolution methods can be employed.

Conflict can be viewed in two different ways. Many of us recognize conflict as something that is bad and should be avoided, but on the flip side, conflict can also be helpful when providing constructive insights, and different ways of thinking should be encouraged as these can provide multiple insights to a problem that is being experienced.

Keep calm

One of the major contributors to conflict is escalation, and this occurs when people start to get angry. When we are angry, we tend to stop listening to what the other person is saying to us and even stop understanding what they are saying. When we are in a heightened state, we also only hear the parts that trigger us in making us argue back.

Taking a step back, keeping calm and looking at the overall situation, not just parts, may help in working towards resolving the situation. Ideally when someone is arguing with you, you need to take that step back and to say to the other person that the conversation needs to stop and you need to take some time to come back and discuss the situation in a calm manner, as arguing often does not find a reasonable resolution.

You also need to realize that most often, conflict will get resolved eventually. You just need to do this in a way that reduces your own anxiety and often the anxiety of the other person too. You also need to consider what is being brought to the situation that you may not be aware of. For example, you or the other person may have had a fight with a partner that morning and the intense feelings inside are spilling over into the current situation. When you feel overwhelmed or have had difficult or painful situations occur outside the current situation, it can make it very hard to stay calm due to frustration and personal hurt.

Good self-advocacy is knowing when to say stop in a conversation that is becoming heated and escalating to conflict. If you know yourself, you know when you are not feeling your best, feel overwhelmed or highly sensitive to an external situation, and then it makes good sense to say to the other person that you need to halt the current conversation so you can take time to gather your thoughts and to centre yourself in a calmer space.

It may also be worthwhile to speak to a friend or, if at work, a close co-worker to help analyse the situation in case you are missing critical points too. Again, this is a good practice in asking for the opinions of others to help you make the right decisions and choices. And remember, they are just giving you their input, they are not there to make the decision for you.

Actively listen to the other person

When reflecting on previous arguments you may have had, ask yourself, how much listening occurred? When replaying these situations, you may realize that you were focused on the parts of the argument that supported your own point or perspective, rather than actively listening to the concerns of the other person and formulating a response that could have de-escalated or resolved the conflict. When we become angry or upset, we often stop listening to the other person's opinions and focus on how we can get our point across. We need to stop and listen carefully and acknowledge the other person's point of view.

Perhaps they will surprise you with their reasoning, or their point is actually true. They may appear to be going on and on about the issue, but until they give an example of how they want to resolve the problem, it can be a very overwhelming experience. In a work context, for instance, they may be bad-mouthing the company's product by insulting people associated with its development, but this is just frustration and anger. When you stop and convey what you want to resolve calmly, you will often get action that will move the situation forward.

When we get angry and upset, it is an emotion usually triggered by anxiety and fear and is also a defence mechanism to protect ourselves. Neurodivergent people often come from a background of fear and anxiety, and finding a way to calmly convey our thoughts and requests can quite surprisingly provide positive outcomes. But let's emphasize here that the other person also needs to listen to help diffuse the anger. If they don't then it will be incredibly difficult to find a positive resolution. Each side needs to be able to vent and let off steam and then calmly work towards a solution. Usually when we are allowed to vent, we feel we are being heard first before solutions are being offered. It is validating rather than making us feel disregarded.

Be considerate when stating your case

This takes some skill and can be quite difficult to do when you are angry or upset. What you need to try and do, if possible, is to gain some composure or take some time to cool down before stating your case. Start by apologizing first if you did do something wrong. This will enable the other person to hear what you have to say next. If you were not at fault, then clearly state everything that occurred that led to the current situation. When details are documented and presented in a calm and clear manner, it leaves no doubt when moving forward in resolving the situation, and you have been active in speaking up to support your case.

Focus on the problem not the person

Rather than attacking or accusing a person, try considering how you convey the problem. You could say something like, 'Let's have a look at why this situation keeps happening.' It is through this process you can ascertain what the problem is, and if it is a person that is part of the problem, they can be addressed through the right processes. In the case of bullying, this needs to be approached with as much documented information as possible, a record kept of times and incidents when this happens, and you should ask colleagues you trust to watch out for you and be a potential witness to the bullying.

Don't focus on the past

This can be incredibly difficult as many neurodivergent people reflect on past negative experiences and have internal negative self-talk. What you need to try and do is focus on how to resolve the problem or situation, learn from that process and use that learning to help yourself move forward. Unpleasant experiences teach you how to approach a difficult and similar situation in the future; next time, you will have prior insight to help you find solutions quickly or avoid it happening again.

Barriers to advocacy

There are a number of barriers to advocacy. These often relate to ableism. Ableism can be from individuals or from society and is prevalent all over the world. Ableism can drive bullying, leading to trauma for neurodivergent people. Anything which invalidates neurodivergent people or gaslights them is a barrier to advocacy. Effective advocacy works best if the advocate likes and values themselves and comes from a place of pride. Therefore, anything that threatens that state of being is a barrier to advocacy.

Ableism and discrimination can occur in a range of settings, including school, further education, the workplace, within families and intimate relationships, in national and international politics, in media representation and in social and online groups. It is hard to be an advocate if you are constantly being put down and invalidated. Conversely, it is easier to advocate for yourself and others if you are in a place of self-love and respect and where you feel proud to be yourself. As such, anything which challenges ableism and discrimination is going to foster a climate where people can advocate for themselves. Advocates fighting against ableism and discrimination are supporting the next generation of advocates through building a place of self-respect and pride.

Building assertiveness skills and setting boundaries

Building assertiveness skills

Assertiveness is one of the most useful tools in the advocate's toolkit. Assertiveness involves being able to say no to people and being able to set boundaries. One of the enemies of assertiveness is under-confidence and being exposed to trauma. Many neurodivergent people struggle to be assertive but it is a really useful skill.

The Better Health Channel ('10 tips for being assertive', 2021), provides the following tips for being assertive:

- Make the decision to positively assert yourself. Commit to being assertive rather than passive or aggressive and start practising today.
- Aim for open and honest communication. Remember to respect other people when you are sharing your feelings, wants, needs, beliefs or opinions.
- Listen actively. Try to understand the other person's point of view and don't interrupt when they are explaining it to you.
- Agree to disagree. Remember that having a different point of view doesn't mean you are right and the other person is wrong.
- Avoid guilt trips. Be honest and tell others how you feel or what you want without making accusations or making them feel guilty.
- Stay calm. Breathe normally, look the person in the eye, keep your face relaxed and speak in a normal voice.
- Take a problem-solving approach to conflict. Try to see the other person as your friend not your enemy.
- Practise assertiveness. Talk in an assertive way in front of a mirror or with a friend. Pay attention to your body language as well as to the words you say.
- Use 'I'. Stick with statements that include 'I' in them such as 'I think' or 'I feel'. Don't use aggressive language such as 'you always' or 'you never'.

- Be patient. Being assertive is a skill that needs practice. Remember that you will sometimes do better at it than at other times, but you can always learn from your mistakes.

These skills can be very difficult to attain but it is possible to build assertiveness capability over time. Assertiveness is a skill which tends to perpetuate itself, so the more you are proactive, the better you get. Being confident, and liking and valuing yourself are great foundations for assertiveness as well. Also, building your self-esteem can help to build your capacity for assertiveness.

Case study: Yenn

I have spent most of my life struggling to be assertive. Bullying at school left me very under-confident, plus my family had never modelled assertiveness. In fact, my parents both really struggle with assertiveness and fear confrontation, so as a kid I never saw anyone being assertive. I figured you just went along with whatever others wanted you to do because confrontation was such a bad thing. I was in my late thirties before I tried to be assertive. The first thing I noticed was that it worked. I didn't have to be rude or mean, just to say what I needed, and the person would do it. It was very enlightening. I also discovered that assertiveness doesn't work with everyone. It definitely doesn't work with sociopaths and narcissists, who seem to thrive on conflict, but thankfully most people are not narcissists! I now practise assertiveness all the time. I can quite happily say no to an opportunity or ask a friend for a favour and not feel guilty or anxious. It is a huge benefit to my advocacy work, and I don't think I could manage my workload without assertiveness. I do wish I had had the capability to be assertive in the past, but I am very glad I can do it now.

Setting boundaries

An important part of advocacy is being able to effectively set boundaries and say no. Advocates are often asked to do things – provide advice, give a presentation, write an article, that sort of thing. Often, we will say yes to these requests, but it is not possible to agree to do everything we are asked and sometimes the best course of action is to say no. Saying no can be really challenging for a variety of reasons. We might worry that if we say no, the person who made the request may not ask us to do anything again. We might worry that our advocacy career will suffer or that we will get a poor reputation because we say no. We might worry that we have upset the person who asked us to do something or that we might never get another opportunity again.

In fact, saying no is an essential skill if you don't want to end up getting burned out and frazzled. Like assertiveness, the capacity to say no often increases with practice. Saying no is good self-care and we can all benefit from doing it. Tell yourself that you need to look out for yourself and saying no to a request is part of that self-care. In the act of saying no, try not to feel guilty. Just explain that you cannot do the thing you are being asked to do. You can say to the person who asked you to do something that you may have capacity at a later date, or you might just say that you are unable to do it, without using any apologies or excuses. You have the right to say no. In fact, saying no is 100 per cent okay. It also means that another advocate might get the opportunity to do something they otherwise wouldn't. So, in reality, saying no is not only helpful for you, it is helpful for the advocacy community as it gives someone else the opportunity to do something. You can also keep a list of colleagues who you can suggest for opportunities that you need to decline.

Learning to say no is one of the most difficult things that neurodivergent people find to do, especially at work. Often neurodivergent people tend to be people pleasers, wanting to do the best they can and wanting to show their worth and value. This can be detrimental to your well-being, especially when you take on too much work due to not saying no.

Due to negative self-talk, overthinking and catastrophizing of situations and previous negative experiences, you may feel pressured into accepting more work than you are effectivity able to handle. This adds to your levels of stress and anxiety and potentially could lead to depression, due to being unable to complete the work you are asked to do.

Also, due to not being able to say no and taking on much more work than you are able to complete, you are essentially eroding your mental well-being, not putting aside enough time for self-care, downtime and doing things that can replenish your energy and help you to do the work effectively.

When you learn to say no, you are creating healthy boundaries for yourself, putting yourself first, and looking after your well-being to ensure that you can continue working in an effective and productive way or can be a good friend or partner. You are realizing your limits and learning to say no when you cannot give any more of yourself.

You need to step away from the misconception that saying no is being uncooperative, selfish or difficult. You also need to realize that by saying no, the consequence will not be that you will no longer be asked to take on tasks, or more concerningly, that you will lose your job.

You may also find it difficult to say no due to the fear of not being liked or accepted as you may have experienced this at school and in many facets of your life. You feel guilty when you say no, assuming that you are letting the employer, the work colleague or your friends down.

So how do you know when to say no?

Saying no is often associated with negativity, but if you continually yes to everything, it can lead to more problems than if you just simply say no. It is critically important to know when to say no, before you become too overwhelmed from taking on too much.

If you keep saying yes, and keep pushing yourself to breaking point, you are setting yourself up for failure, with incomplete tasks or doing your tasks half-heartedly or carelessly. This can potentially erode your self-esteem and value if this keeps happening over and over again.

What you need to do is think it through. Where possible, don't answer the request straightaway. Ask your employer or work colleague to give you some time to think it through and get back to them, as you want to check your schedule and check how much work you currently have. Ask them when this needs to be done by and then assess if you have the time to take on what they are asking, and to your usual standards.

Remember, if you don't work to your own expectations and personal standards, this can also add to your stress and affect how you feel about yourself.

You also need to ask yourself how long it will take you to do the task, and what the deadline is for completion, as this can affect other jobs that you are currently undertaking. When you take the time to ask yourself these questions, you gain a realistic idea as to whether you can complete this work on time and to your best ability.

Also, when you ask yourself these questions you can then analyse to see if you are being stretched too far, and if other tasks are a priority. As you self-assess through asking these questions, assessing your current workload, it will become obvious if you can or cannot take on more work.

You will then have the answer to the question, which may well be no, I cannot take on more work at this time.

And this goes for any situation, not just in the workplace. It applies to what you do in your own time, in your home life, with family and friends. The more you understand your capacity, the easier it becomes for you to identify how much you can do and when you need to say no.

How do we learn to say no in a positive way?

First, let's look at how to do this at work.

Depending on your preferred communication method, whether you prefer to speak directly to your work colleagues or your manager, or if you prefer to send an email, you need to explain your current situation and why you cannot take on further work. Recognizing your best way of communication can also have an impact on how you convey your response.

For example, emails can be easily misconstrued due to the tone of your responses perceived by the other person. To you, it may sound as if you are being clear and direct, but to the receiver it may appear unfriendly or abrupt.

Be careful in how you convey this information. For example, don't start out by stating how much work you already have on, how overworked you are, and that you feel they are being inconsiderate by not understanding or knowing this. This can come across in a passive-aggressive way.

Instead, first thank the manager or the work colleague for considering you for the task and then explain to them that you are unable to take on this project and give your best to it and your full focus to complete it in the timeframe they have requested.

You can also explain to the employer or work colleague your current priorities and how important it is to get those tasks that you've already committed to done efficiently and well.

Prioritizing tasks and when to decline extra work

If you have difficulty in prioritizing tasks and identifying which task is most important, ask for support. If your job consists of multiple tasks, ask your employer or work colleague to break it down and explain which tasks are most important and are therefore a priority.

Asking for clarification will help reduce anxiety and negative internal self-talk because you will understand and know what is expected of you. A good employer will welcome open and honest communication. When you are asking for support or clarification, this should not be viewed as a negative but as a positive skill, and taking initiative in helping you understand the tasks and expectations.

Suffering in silence is detrimental to your well-being and by asking for support and clarification, you are inadvertently implementing self-care, reducing the unknown and your anxieties, and improving your self-esteem and self-confidence through doing your job well and to expectations.

Open communication can positively identify prioritization of tasks and encourage you to schedule and plan for the day, week or month ahead. Many neurodivergent people thrive on clear instruction, planning and having schedules. This is a must in the workplace, at school and at home, and important to add to your self-care toolbox.

Providing suggestions and solutions

Another way of saying no is to find an alternative solution for your employer's or colleague's request.

You may be able to ask for help from one of your work colleagues or suggest a work colleague who you know doesn't currently have a significantly heavy workload and may be able to take on the task.

You may know another colleague who may be more suited to the job that is being requested of you. By suggesting this person to take on the job, you are finding potential solutions to the situation, encouraging good communication and thinking of ways to resolve the situation by finding a suitable outcome that will help get the job done.

Also, asking the person if there is some flexibility in when the task needs to be done or if your current workload can be changed to accommodate the new task is also a good way to help problem-solve the situation.

Learning how to avoid fatigue

Saying no also is applicable outside work

We often find ourselves saying yes to many stressful situations when in reality we would rather say no. For example, you have had a big day at work and are feeling overwhelmed and tired due to sensory overload from the bright lights and noise at work, and you're looking forward to a night in with your pet cat, watching Netflix. But the workplace is having a social meet-up with drinks at the local noisy pub so people can get to know their colleagues better, or the office has organized an online Zoom drinks and virtual beach party that requires you to turn up your heating if you are in the northern hemisphere and have loud 80s music playing while you all dance and chat virtually... It's overwhelming just thinking about that scenario!

Anyway, for many neurodivergent people this is the last thing they feel like doing and strikes fear into their souls and adds more pressure to their already stressed selves. The thought of more sensory bombardment through loud music and talking and now more screen time seems like torture, rather than a fun night with work colleagues.

Unfortunately, due to the fact that many neurodivergent people feel the need to fit in and to be accepted by their peers, they will force themselves into these situations, often setting themselves up for disaster through more stress, anxiety, mental fatigue and potential meltdown.

In situations like this you need to ascertain how you can say no without the fear of rejection from your peers. Depending on the situation, how overwhelmed, tired or stressed you may be will give an indicator as to whether you should attend and if you do decide to do so, how long for.

You need to effectively plan your escape when you are asked to social events and know how to positively serve your well-being. This is another tool in implementing self-care to add to your toolbox of healthy strategies.

If you are up to it, you can tell your colleagues or friends that you can come along for the pre-dinner drinks if in person, or attend online for say an hour, and then have to leave due to other commitments at home. This commitment can be you have a date with your cat and Netflix. You don't have to elaborate to your colleagues what you will be doing, just that you can only attend for a short amount of time due to another commitment.

This will be perceived by colleagues as you making an effort in being part of the team, but it is on your terms. And your motivator for leaving and not being persuaded into staying longer than you want to is that thought of curling up with your kitty watching the latest series on Netflix. You see, this is an easy way to keep yourself motivated! Win-win!

You should never feel obligated or pressured into having to explain your reasons for leaving early, nor feel pressured into doing something that you know will make you feel uncomfortable or is detrimental to your well-being. We all have different levels of how much we can cope with and that is completely fine.

Again, these strategies also work with family gatherings, catching up with friends and hanging out with school friends. You choose how long and how often. And stick to it. You will thank yourself for knowing your limits and being firm in how long you will attend.

The consequences of too much socializing – social hangovers

One of the things we can often experience the next day, if we do take on too many things and socialize for too long or past our limits, is a social hangover. A social hangover is the feeling of utter depletion, being incredibly tired and exhausted from too much socializing.

Some other feelings that we may have are irritability, anger or having difficulty in concentrating, with symptoms being quite similar to those when we drink too much alcohol – hence the term social hangover.

We feel as if our mind is sluggish, we are irritable, and we certainly do not want to talk to anyone as we have been socializing and talking and listening to people talking too much the previous day. All we want is to be left alone to either stay in bed and sleep, or just watch TV until we can actually start feeling better about ourselves and as if we can function again.

Also, it can take some time to recover from a social hangover. Generally, most people after a social event don't feel too tired and usually only need the usual amount of sleep and feel better again in the morning. Or they can actually feel energized from socializing!

But for many neurodivergent people, due to the multiple sensory bombardment and overwhelm of the occasion, plus any overstimulation from the day and/or week prior to the event, it can take up to a week or more to recover.

So, be mindful of how much you can tolerate in any social situation. Identify your limits and use this knowledge to support your well-being.

Recovery

As previously discussed, be firm in saying no if you are already overwhelmed, or just commit a small amount of time to the social event you have been asked to attend. Prevention and self-care are always better than trying to recover.

Now, to recover from a social hangover you need to be kind to yourself. You need to realize that you cannot make any fast or rash decisions when you are not feeling your best. Allow your body and mind to heal and recover from the overwhelming situation you have experienced.

Resisting, or not taking the time for self-care that you need for recovery, will only make things worse. You can become more stressed, irritable and anxious, potentially leading to a major meltdown, a breakdown or depression.

So how can you recover from this overstimulation? Put simply, you need to do whatever your body is asking you. If you feel that you need to sleep in all day, then do it. If you just want to sit and watch TV or read books, then do it. If you feel you need to take a long walk in nature alone, then do it. Do whatever it takes to refill your energy during this recovery phase. You are not being lazy or selfish, you are taking care of you and implementing good self-care.

You need to realize and analyse what will help you to recover from social situations. When you take the time to reflect and analyse what has caused you to feel so overwhelmed, what you felt in that situation, you can learn how to best recover from it.

Also, once you learn to identify what overwhelms you, you can learn how to avoid it or at least lessen the effects from future overwhelming situations. If you know your limits, you can prepare yourself before a situation arises. For example, if there is a social situation in two weeks' time, implement a plan a week prior to that event so that you can be prepared as best you can to cope with it. Take extra time for self-care. Take extra time out for yourself, or spend more time alone prior to the event so you are mentally prepared for the social gathering.

This could be things like not watching any TV, spending lots of time in quiet places and not meeting with other people. Or reading a book or taking a hot shower or bath. Ideally, do activities that will give you back energy so you can build up a surplus to carry you through the upcoming draining event or activity.

By learning what your sensory triggers are, you can also plan during that week prior to the event to reduce sensory impact as much as possible. For example, if you have sensory aversions to cleaning products, avoid doing any major cleaning until after the event and after you have recovered.

If you get overwhelmed by bright lights, ensure that you wear tinted glasses or sunglasses whenever possible to reduce sensory stress. Spend extra time in nature or with your furry companion. Again, fill up prior to the event on energy-giving activities so you have more energy to help you cope with the impending draining situation.

Energy accounting or spoon theory
Some of you may have heard of energy accounting or another term called spoon theory. They both aim to help us identify what takes away energy and how we can replenish energy.

Energy accounting is taking the time to write up a list of what drains our energy, which is called withdrawals, and another list that replenishes our energy, which is called deposits. A numerical value is added to each of the withdrawals and deposits to identify how much energy each of these gives or takes away.

The concept is that when a withdrawal or multiple withdrawals are made, deposits also need to be made to keep the energy levels in balance and avoid energy levels running into the negative, which can lead to exhaustion, overwhelm and meltdown.

This concept was developed by Maja Toudal in Denmark as a tool to help her organize her energy while going through school. This tool can be really useful for neurodivergent people as our energy levels vary considerably differently from typical people. We often lose a lot of energy in social situations, whereas typical people can feel energized from these very same situations that drain us. We need to be able to identify how much energy we are losing so we can implement good self-care by adding more energy-replenishing activities into our daily lives. When we actually see what is draining and replenishing, it can become quite clear and, in some cases, quite surprising at just how much energy we are continually losing and not refilling.

Spoon theory came from a personal story by Christine Miderandino who has a chronic autoimmune disease, Lupus, and wanted her friend to better understand the reality of what it was like living with this. This theory describes the amount of physical and/or mental energy a person has available each day to do everyday tasks, including energy to spend time with other people. The visual representation of spoons, with each spoon being a unit of energy, helps give the person an idea of how much energy they will need to do daily things and how much energy they are also losing. Often when people use this representation, they find that they are running out of spoons or have no spoons left to do any further activities. So, this visual representation helps people to identify what is using up their spoons and to find activities to replace the spoons they are using.

Burnout

The compounding factors of exhaustion from socialization, struggling to say no, feeling devalued or misunderstood at work, school or by family and friends, along with sensory overwhelm and triggers, and not knowing our limits and not implementing good self-care can all lead to high levels of anxiety, depression and, potentially, burnout.

When we are continually impacted by negative or draining experiences, we are setting ourselves up for burnout. When we are in burnout, we feel extremely tired and exhausted, and suffer from mental fatigue and brain fog. We have increased levels of irritability and we cannot cope with people talking to us or with socializing with other people.

Our levels of anxiety increase significantly due to our overwhelm and reduced capacity to work or do usual tasks. Along with this increased anxiety, we also become highly sensitive to the sensory bombardment that we already experience in our lives. These high levels make it extremely difficult to function and concentrate, adding to our mental fatigue even more.

We can also experience a decrease in sensory information, so experiences that may have been pleasing or invigorating to us in the past no longer fulfil us or re-energize us. This is particularly apparent when our intense interests no longer fulfil us or give us the energy back that we so desperately need. This is also an indicator that we may be bordering on or are in depression. But note that depression is distinctively different to burnout.

We can also experience a decrease in our language skills, including communication through written means, and this can be seen by a decrease in our usual interactions that we may have on social media or we no longer text or keep in contact with family or friends. It can also be apparent by the length of what we write or convey. This can be significantly reduced when we are in burnout. These are all signs that we are becoming withdrawn and turning inwards to protect ourselves from further overwhelm and all are desperate coping mechanisms once we hit burnout. We literally shut down.

When in burnout we may experience increased shutdowns and meltdowns and the length and frequency and severity of these also increase. Furthermore, burnout contributes to our reduced ability to self-regulate our emotions and feelings. When we are overwhelmed, tired, irritable and depressed, we find it extremely difficult to keep our emotional state intact. We are using every ounce of our energy in keeping it all together.

The increasing overwhelm and exhaustion also have a significant impact on our thinking. We find it increasingly difficult to use our mental capacity to think more than just how to survive the day. We have significant difficulty with things like abstract thought and problem-solving, which may have come to us easily in the past.

This reduced capacity and feeling of inability to what seem like simple tasks add to our sense of guilt that we are not able to do the things that we used to do. Also, when we are extremely overwhelmed and exhausted, we become more forgetful.

There will also be an increase in executive dysfunction, so along with forgetting things we need to do, we may miss appointments, may not be able to complete the tasks, may not know how to start or do a task, and task inertia – the ability to be able to start a project or task – becomes increasingly prevalent. It all contributes to the overwhelm.

An interesting thing to note is that there is also an increase in demand avoidance. This is where we feel so overwhelmed when someone asks to do something that we resist and avoid these demands on us. We may find excuses, have uncontrollable outbursts or moods swings because we are at our limit or capacity and find it incredibly difficult to explain to the other person that we quite simply cannot do what they are asking.

Burnout and advocacy

Advocacy comes with some attached challenges. One of these is burnout. Burnout happens when we take on too many things or when we are overloaded over a period of time. Overload can be social, work-related, emotional, sensory or a combination of many things. Burnout can creep up on you. If you are passionate about advocacy, then burnout can be a major risk. This is due to people taking on more and more things because they feel so strongly about making a difference. A lot of positive feedback about your work can lead to you taking on more and more things and then before you know it you can find yourself experiencing burnout.

Burnout is not the sole domain of autistic or neurodivergent people, but it often affects us to a greater extent. This can be because we don't see it coming and by the time it hits, we are overwhelmed. It can also be due to us being more affected by overload than others.

There are some early warning signs of burnout. If you find yourself feeling stressed about tasks which you would normally be enthusiastic about, that can be a sign of impending burnout. If you feel stressed or uncomfortable when you are given an opportunity for advocacy – or other work which you usually enjoy – that is a warning sign. If you have more overload, meltdowns and shutdowns than usual then that can be a sign.

If you are getting burned out the best thing to do is stop. Decline opportunities, say no to new tasks. Don't worry, someone else can usually do whatever you have declined. If you can head off burnout before it gets too bad then that is a great outcome.

Case study: Yenn

In 2015, I had a major episode of burnout. My advocacy career was taking off and I was very excited about it. I took on dozens of opportunities and was absolutely delighted. At the same time, I was mentoring a young autistic man. He was very angry and negative and also kept asking me sexual questions. I found myself getting stressed every time I interacted with this man. I was not so good at assertiveness so couldn't set a boundary. Every time my phone beeped with a message my anxiety would go off the scale. I went to Brisbane for a conference and while normally I love conferences, at this one I just felt exhausted and reluctant to even be there. I ended up blocking the young man and had a couple of months off tasks. I had to take a lot of downtime and it was a very difficult period. I now take planned downtime every day and say no to doing things which I know will be too much.

Burnout and depression

It has been considered that burnout is a syndrome that develops in response to adverse working conditions. As discussed, these include mental exhaustion, reduced work capacity and accomplishments. At the core of burnout is the emotional exhaustion people experience due to reduced capacity to complete tasks and to self-regulate emotions. Burnout can coincide with depression and is often a precursor to developing depression.

Removing or limiting the contact you have with people

If family or friends are making your life difficult, are not supportive of you, or if they refuse to acknowledge your neurological difference or diagnosis, then you really need to consider whether you need these people in your life and if they are actually supporting you.

When family and friends don't acknowledge your neurological differences, how you think and how you do things, that you need downtime and more self-care than typical people, they are in essence adding to your mental distress.

You can use up enormous amounts of energy in trying to figure out ways you can make them understand you and how they can support you. But quite often they are not ready or not prepared to understand or support you.

They may come out with things like, 'We already know you and it doesn't matter if you have a diagnosis or not', without considering that you want them to learn about you and how you have struggled, frequently silently and alone, and you would like them to truly understand who you are and how to support you. It can be incredibly tiring and mentally draining. It is also devaluing who you are, especially when they don't believe the constant struggles and barriers you have experienced for many years.

If they are not prepared to learn about you and your neurology, and especially if it has been some time since your diagnosis, then you need to decide if you want to continue having them in your life and if you do, how much time you wish to spend with them.

So, reduce the amount of time that you spend with the people who do not support or acknowledge your needs or cause you distress, especially by dismissing or invalidating you. You can still tell these people that you love them, and care for them, especially if they are your parents or siblings, and that you're doing your best, but you need to cut down on the amount of time you will spend with them because you want to look after your mental well-being and do what's best for you.

This is also about saying no to situations that cause you distress and again setting firm boundaries. When we set boundaries, we are setting ourselves up to look after our own well-being by drawing a line and saying, 'This is what I will accept, and this is how I want my life to be. If you do not support or fully accept who I am, then I need to put these boundaries in place to help me to look after me and to enable me to be the best version of myself.'

When you set boundaries, you also need to stick to them. When you stick to your boundaries, you are looking after yourself and implementing good self-care.

Special occasions

Special occasions, like birthdays, religious holidays, Mother's Day and Father's Day, especially with family and friends, can often bring up thoughts of dread, anxiety, depression and exclusion. Many people can find these days quite difficult and overwhelming and can feel quite lonely at these particular times. Quite often, we feel left out or on the outside in these situations due to previous negative, traumatic or over-whelming experiences that have occurred when we have attended them in the past.

So, what you can do in these situations is to do something special for yourself. This could be engaging in your favourite interest or spending time with people who get you and support you. This can be either via gatherings in person or meeting up with people online. On religious holidays, it can also be worthwhile checking out if there is a local charity event you could help out at that may give you the opportunity to meet other people.

Gaining self-confidence and resilience

This section looks at how to build resilience and self-confidence, both of which are critical skills for an advocate.

Building self-confidence

Self-confidence is at the heart of advocacy, but it can be difficult to build. Some strategies to help with this include:

- Spend time with supportive neurodivergent peers and friends.
- Reflect on your achievements. Make a list of all the things you're proud of in your life. Add to the list with more accomplishments. They don't need to be earth-shattering achievements, just things you have done that make you feel good about yourself. Refer to the list when you doubt yourself.
- Think of things you're good at. Everyone has strengths and talents. Remind yourself of yours.
- Set some goals. Outline the steps you need to take to achieve these. They don't have to be big goals.
- Positive self-talk. You're never going to feel confident if you have negative commentary running through your mind telling you that you're no good. Think about your self-talk and how that might be affecting your self-confidence.

- Follow your passion/interest. Many neurodivergent people have a passion or interest that they love. Following your passion is a great way to build your confidence.
- Affirm yourself. This is a great way to help build self-confidence. When you find yourself saying or thinking negative things about yourself, challenge this and replace it with something affirming.
- Care for yourself. This is a practical way of building self-confidence. Do something each day to care for yourself. Treat yourself to a small gift to mark occasions and accomplishments.

Self-confidence doesn't happen overnight, but it can be a great boost to your advocacy efforts as it puts you in a position where you have the capacity to stand up for yourself. Successes in advocacy can also boost your self-confidence.

Building resilience

Resilience is an important quality for life and particularly for advocacy. Resilience enables a person to manage adversity and setbacks, to 'fail successfully' in order to navigate life well. Resilient people find it easier to take risks and put themselves in a position where there may be challenges – qualities that advocates benefit from. Going through a journey of advocacy helps people to build their resilience so it is win-win.

One way of approaching resilience is to see that there are three main elements to it: the place of safety, controlled challenges and failing successfully.

The place of safety refers to an environment of love and care where people are respected and valued. It more typically relates to children and a family environment but can also refer to friends and partners fostering confidence and positivity. Coming from the background of a place of safety helps scaffold a person's confidence and capacity for resilience. It is easier to find confidence in yourself and take on challenges and risks if you come from a place of support.

Controlled challenges are the engine room of resilience. These challenges can be a range of things and going through them helps to build a person's confidence to take on similar challenges, meaning that they can do more and more difficult things. Resilience works like a muscle being strengthened through exercise. Incrementally more difficult challenges strengthen that muscle, making resilience easier to achieve. An example of this for an advocate would be to build in slightly more challenging activities around their advocacy work. A person might want to build their profile and influence on social media. A controlled challenge might involve them posting in some autism groups and then maybe taking on a more challenging activity like creating a page for their own advocacy work. A further controlled challenge might involve them responding to questions and comments on their page. Building in controlled challenges enables us to increase our confidence in taking on things which are difficult and can increase our skill level.

Failing successfully is exactly what it sounds like – using setbacks and failure to learn skills and be able to manage setbacks in the future. There is an attitude around failure which is more likely to make it a positive and that is the attitude that failure and setbacks produce experience, knowledge and wisdom. An example of this for an advocate might involve their attitude around an error. For instance, a meeting with a health practitioner might have gone badly due to assumptions and miscommunication. The advocate might use the experience to learn how they could have a similar conversation in a different and more effective way. In this instance, the 'failure' may not have been due to an error on the part of the advocate but they can still use the experience in order to learn for similar situations in the future.

All three elements of building resilience can be challenging but they can work well and help boost the capability for resilience which in turn supports the capacity for advocacy. We can view resilience as a way to use difficulties, mistakes and setbacks to increase our understanding of the world and our ability to navigate life, both as advocates and as human beings. Resilience is essentially the act of harnessing the challenges we inevitably will face in order to make us more skilled and confident in facing the world.

Case study: Yenn

In 2012, I met a young autistic man. We will call him Adam. Anyone who has been to one of my talks on employment, education or resilience will probably have heard this story. When I told Adam I was autistic, worked full-time in government administration and – at that point – had one published book, he said, 'You're lying. That isn't possible.' I was keen to defend my integrity but then realized that in Adam's world at least, an autistic person couldn't do those things. Adam and his parents had been given a deficits-based view and it was clear Adam had not been allowed to undertake all that many things which challenged him. At 21 he had a year nine education and had not engaged in any study in the preceding six years. He had been receiving the disability pension as soon as he was eligible, at the age of 16. I saw Adam and felt for him. I thought that he had been done a big disservice by all the deficits thinking, the fear that if something was hard, he would be upset or have a meltdown, which must be avoided at all cost. It was almost as if the things that had been done with the intention of caring for him and making his life more pleasant as a child had in fact backfired. At the time I met Adam, I had always believed that an early autism diagnosis was a positive thing, helping autistic young people know their identity and get the supports they needed to navigate the world. But the only world Adam navigated was his bedroom and the virtual worlds of online games. I did not criticize Adam and I knew that life is complicated, and people can struggle to engage with the world for a number of reasons. But I also wanted to help create a world in which autistic young people could be proud of who they are and take on and overcome the challenges they need to do to engage in life in the best way for them. At that moment of realization, my work in advocacy began in earnest.

I interpreted the main issues Adam was facing as a lack of being allowed to take on challenges and risks and to be supported through those. The primary issue in my mind was that lack of capacity for resilience was holding Adam back. This became a big motivator for me and still is what drives my passion. My *Wonderful World of Work* book (2014) was written as a direct means of addressing the issue I saw around resilience and autism.

Resilience to me is about being able to take on challenges, work through them and come out the other side with confidence and mastery. And that confidence and mastery can translate across and into other challenges and areas of life. This is not a quick process and it does not stand alone. Things like self-esteem, confidence and independence are all related to resilience.

One thing to clear up about resilience though. When someone tells me that someone – usually an educator – has told them that their autistic child will not be bullied if they 'get some resilience', it makes my blood boil. The person saying that is not speaking about resilience or anything close to it. What they are doing is dismissing and invalidating that child's experience; they are blaming the victim. No matter how a child became a bully, the victim of that bully's poor behaviour is not responsible for the bullying behaviour in any way. That is *not* resilience.

Genuine resilience has a range of benefits for autistic children and adults.

I am interested in this for a number of reasons, in addition to Adam. One of them is that I used a process of controlled challenges to build my own capacity to work after being outside the labour force for almost ten years in my early adult life. I didn't articulate or understand that I was 'doing resilience' and it was quite intuitive – it just seemed like a good approach at the time! I went from having a severe experience of perfectionism at a dishwashing job, resulting in mental health issues requiring hospital treatment. My issue was the perceived level of responsibility at work. Even though the worst mistake I could make in the dishwashing job would probably have been to send a dirty fork out, in my mind if I had screwed up, the whole business would have gone bust. At the time this was happening I didn't for one moment think I would never be able to work, despite that seeming the likely outcome of my problematic work history. Instead, I thought *I can't work now, at this moment in time.* In the next five years, I built my work resilience by working as a volunteer in a gallery, building confidence from that to having a very small business doing video editing for my art school colleagues, building confidence from that to work in a charity and then after six months of that and the publication of my first book, moving on to a full-time professional role. I had built my resilience for work from being terrified of the tiniest amount of responsibility to working in a corporate role with lots of responsibility. I have been in my corporate workplace for almost 11 years now and have even more responsibility at work and in my advocacy work too. I rarely think about the responsibility, I just do what I need to do.

This should be seen in the context of challenges faced by autistic people in completing study and finding work. This example shows me managing my individual issues with work though resilience. However, there are also broader social issues and disadvantages which my getting a job didn't and couldn't overcome. Addressing these issues does require a broader approach than expecting individual autistic people to work through their individual challenges.

Building your self-confidence and resilience is a good way to build a basis and foundation for your advocacy practice. While it can be difficult to do, the rewards can be immense.

Stages of life

Neurodivergent people go through a number of life stages where the need for advocacy and the kind of advocacy required will most likely be different. It is important to note that these age brackets are a guideline only and some people will not fit neatly within the descriptors.

Primary school

Young children will almost certainly need a parent or carer to advocate on their behalf at this age. Some older children will do some of their own advocacy and some young children are engaged in the neurodiversity movement, but generally advocacy will happen on behalf of the child and be driven by their parent or carer to start off with. It is important to be aware that children have the right to advocacy and in fact have the same rights that adults have. Advocacy needs to be inclusive of and based on the child's wishes. The child needs to be at the centre of advocacy, even if they cannot fully articulate their needs. Advocacy is about the child, not the parent or other adults. Advocacy needs to be done in consultation with the child wherever possible. If a child does not use verbal speech, they can still be engaged in advocacy discussions via augmentative and alternative technology (AAC) (for example, *Proloquo2Go*). Some areas where advocacy for young children can take place include childcare settings, school, healthcare settings, in friendships and in relationships with family/extended family.

Advocacy for primary school age children is generally done by parents. Here are some issues which can occur in primary school:

- Bullying by other students. Many neurodivergent students are bullied by their peers. Bullying can be overt or covert and frequently results in trauma. Neurodivergent students may fight back against bullies, resulting in them being disciplined. It is often the case that bullies carry out their bullying away from the eyes of school staff but the neurodivergent student retaliating does so in full view of authorities. Staff may be unaware there was an issue and judge the neurodivergent student as needlessly violent based on their response to bullying. The bullying may have been going on for an extended period of time and the response is desperate.

- Bullying by staff. Teachers and school staff can be bullies themselves. This is particularly problematic for the student and their parents. Any complaint is likely to be dismissed, leaving the student feeling powerless and defeated. School staff may close ranks if a complaint is made against one of their number.

- Inflexible education practices. Schools often have rules which appear to exist entirely for the sake of having rules. Neurodivergent students can struggle with adhering to rules which seem arbitrary and pointless. Flexibility is key for helping neurodivergent students to shine, so rules for the sake of rules need to be addressed. Sometimes school staff are unaware that inflexibility exists, so advocacy is around removing them.

- Discipline for things like stimming. Some schools will discipline neurodivergent students for doing things which are part of self-regulation and are not hurting anyone, such as stimming. Discipline for self-regulation is not helpful and if anything will leave neurodivergent students doubting and feeling bad about themselves. Advocacy in this area needs to be around building the knowledge and understanding of school staff and helping them to see that self-regulation is a positive thing.

- Educational methods which are punitive. Some schools view neurodivergent students as 'naughty' or poorly behaved. In fact, neurodivergent kids do whatever behaviour they do in order to communicate something. Punishing students for 'poor' behaviour is much less effective than discovering why the child has done the behaviour and addressing the root cause. Advocacy in this space needs to be about educating the school staff and advising them of the child's reason for doing what they are doing, if known.

- School not listening to parents. Some schools do not listen to the parents of neurodivergent students and see them as the enemy. This is a difficult situation and may require mediation or even changing schools if it becomes entrenched.

- Responses to meltdown. If a child has a meltdown at school this can be seen in a number of ways by school staff, including that it is poor behaviour or a tantrum in order to force an outcome. In reality, meltdowns are not the same as tantrums. They are a response due to overload, rather than something done in order to force a response (as a tantrum would be). Advocacy in this area could involve talking to school staff about triggers for meltdown and also de-escalation strategies which might work for the child.
- 'Gifted and talented' programmes which downplay challenges. Some gifted and talented programmes do not fully understand the challenges that neurodivergent kids have. Functioning labels are often used and children in these programmes are seen as needing minimal support due to being 'gifted'.
- Negative attitudes of other parents towards the neurodivergent child. Some parents are hostile to neurodivergent children and see them as disruptive. Some parents even think the neuro-divergence is not real and children are just poorly behaved. Advocacy in this space can involve speaking with the parents individually to help them understand life for neurodivergent children.

Neurodivergent children may or may not be aware of these issues, meaning that parents themselves may not know that there is an issue. It is important to encourage children to raise issues with parents as much as possible. In some cases, parents can work through issues and how to address them with their children.

High school

The teen/high school years often involve both the parent/carer and the teen themselves doing advocacy. Once again, advocacy is for and about the teen, not the parent, the school or anyone else. If a teen does not use verbal speech, they can still be engaged in advocacy dis-cussions via AAC. Teens may require some guidance and support in order to advocate for themselves. Instilling a sense of agency, positive self-knowledge and pride in teens can support them to learn to advo-cate for themselves. The kinds of settings where teens may have a need for advocacy include being at school, in friendships, relationships with family, coming to an understanding of their gender and their sexuality and emergent independence.

Many of the issues encountered in primary school also occur in high school. The main difference is that by high school, neurodivergent students generally have more capability to advocate for themselves. This advocacy may be supported by parents and carers. The challenges at high school can be seen as a good opportunity for neurodivergent children and teens to build their knowledge and confidence of advocacy. There are some organizations that support and mentor autistic students, including the I CAN Network in Australia.

Here are some issues encountered in high school:

- Bullying by peers. There are similar considerations for this issue as in primary school.
- Bullying by staff. There are similar considerations for this issue as in primary school.
- Gender diversity and identity issues. It is important to note that this can also occur in the primary years. Many autistic young people are trans and gender diverse. There are a range of issues which trans and gender diverse young people face and there is a lot of hatred and transphobia levelled at these young people. Advocacy can involve standing up to bigots and working with school staff to support acceptance and respect. Gender diverse young people can be very vulnerable and can benefit from the support of allies – these can be their parents or someone else who supports them, such as a friend.
- Trans and gender diverse young people and neurodivergent young people are at higher risks for suicidal ideation and mental illness, so advocacy and support in this space are really important.

Case study: Kai

Kai is 14 and has a diagnosis of ADHD. Kai is non-binary and came out 12 months ago to their friend at school and then two weeks later to their parents. Kai is very honest and up front in their communication. They had been questioning their gender identity for some months and when they came out they were very clear and confident that they were non-binary. Kai's father was very supportive, but their mother did not take their coming out well. She said that Kai could not know their gender as a teenager and that they were just going through a phase. She also said that Kai's ADHD affected their judgement and that they couldn't know their gender. Understandably, this led to Kai feeling very upset and not supported. Kai became quite depressed. Their father tried to help but the rejection by their mother was just too hurtful. Kai's dad was really worried about them and made an appointment with their psychologist. Thankfully, Kai's mum came around to understanding that Kai needed her to be supportive and that it could actually be dangerous to Kai's health and well-being if she was not. She did some research about gender diversity and neurodivergence and apologized to Kai. While things aren't entirely fixed, Kai and their mum are getting along better and Kai feels more accepted and respected.

- Challenges with academic study. Many neurodivergent young people struggle with academic learning, be they dyslexic, autistic or have ADHD. Exam stress or homework and struggling with how the information is presented and the teaching style can make life at school difficult. These issues can result in students being seen as underachievers and can impact on their self-esteem and self-respect. Advocacy in this space can involve talking to educators about the specific issues faced by neurodivergent young people and working out strategies to help them learn well and navigate things like exams and study. Advocacy from parents and carers should also involve building the self-confidence of young people and helping them to understand their value and that they are not somehow deficient or failing.
- Mental health issues. Neurodivergent young people are more at risk of mental health issues than the general population. This often takes the form of depression or anxiety disorders but can be any of the mental health diagnoses. Mental health issues often show up in adolescence and can impact on transition points such as high school to further education, or work transitions. They also put young people at greater risk of suicide. There is more information on mental health advocacy later in this book.

Further education

Issues which can arise in further education and where advocacy can be beneficial include:

- Relationships with other students. Some students may be ableist or hostile. Others may be too 'hands on' and want more from a friendship than the neurodivergent person does. Social settings in further education can be very challenging. It is often about assertiveness and setting boundaries with others.
- Relationships with academic staff. There are some unwritten rules around relationships with academic staff. Generally, they are not viewed as friends and the relationship is professional. Being too friendly with academic staff can be misinterpreted as there being favouritism or cronyism happening, even where it isn't. If a situation arises where there is such a misinterpretation then advocacy may involve explaining what the actual situation is to anyone who thinks favouritism is happening.
- Issues with coursework. Coursework can be a challenge for neurodivergent people for a variety of reasons, including work differing from high school, the way the tuition is delivered or anxiety around exams or completing the coursework. Neurodivergent students may struggle academically and require advocacy to explain why there is an issue. Assuming the academic staff will understand why there is an issue is unhelpful. Advocacy in this instance may involve explaining the issue with academic staff and working together to find a solution.
- Sensory issues in built environments. Sensory issues in the built environment can be immense and mean that neurodivergent students cannot attend classes. Once again, advocacy in this space will most likely involve explaining the issue to academic staff and working together to find a solution. For example, there is one autistic university lecturer who has major issues with glare and lights and so wears a baseball cap when delivering lectures to address their sensory issues.
- Independent learning. Some neurodivergent people have difficulties transitioning from school and the level of academic support there to further education, which involves more

independent learning. These students can struggle. Advocacy here can be around explaining to academic staff that there is an issue and working together to support the student to be better able to manage independent learning.

- Unfair treatment from staff. Academic staff can be – or be perceived to be – unfair at times. This is a difficult situation but one which requires addressing. Advocacy can involve taking up the issue with the staff member involved or going to their supervisor. Advocacy may also involve contacting the student union. This is potentially a very sensitive area and it may be beneficial to seek some advice on how to proceed.
- Group work. Group work with fellow students can be problematic if others let the neurodivergent student do all the work and then benefit from the mark they get which the other students have not contributed to. This can require assertiveness during the course work but it can be very stressful.
- Credit for work. People can take credit for others' work in further education. While it is not permitted, it still happens on occasion. It is a fraught area and can have serious consequences. Once again, this is an area where it may be advisable to seek the opinion and advice of a trusted friend or family member.

In the workplace

There are issues which can arise in the workplace and require advocacy:

- Sensory issues. Even if the neurodivergent person's job is enjoyable and their managers and colleagues supportive, sensory issues can make employment very challenging and, in some cases, impossible. Advocacy in this space often revolves around speaking with the manager or Human Resources department to address the sensory issues. Sensory issues come under the umbrella of accessibility, so the workplace needs to make the job accessible. However, it can be hard to communicate sensory needs to an HR manager who does not understand the issues. It can be best to describe how you feel when in sensory overload.
- Bullying. This is a big problem for workplaces, and autistic employees can be victims of it. Bullying can make a job that was initially loved absolutely unbearable. Bullying needs to be

addressed but it can be hard to do so. It can definitely be hard to advocate against bullying alone. Some workplaces have HR departments who can assist with addressing bullying. It can be hard to address the bully directly about their behaviour so it may be worth involving a third party such as the bully's manager. It can help to vent to a trusted person but be aware that venting alone is unlikely to solve the issue. Sometimes the only way to address workplace bullying is to leave the position where the bullying took place. While that is totally unfair and seems as if the bully has 'won', it can be a survival strategy.

- Relationships with managers. The relationship with your manager is probably the most important relationship you will have at work. A positive relationship will make work that much easier and more enjoyable, but a difficult relationship may mean work is unpleasant and stressful. Advocacy can involve explaining your needs to your manager and talking about autism if you feel comfortable to do so.

- Relationships with colleagues. The colleague relationship is also very important. You work with your colleagues every day and you may work together with them to do joint projects, so it is important that you get along well. Advocacy can involve talking to your colleagues about your needs and being assertive around the allocation of tasks in group work. Advocacy can also involve going to your manager if there is an issue with colleagues or, if you are able to, talking to the colleague directly.

- Navigating unwritten rules. Neurodivergent employees often struggle with unwritten rules in the workplace – things like making small talk, knowing what clothes to wear and etiquette around after-work events. Advocacy can involve explaining to managers and colleagues that you have different approaches to unwritten rules and asking questions if you are confused. It can also involve talking about autism if that is something you are comfortable to do. Advocacy can also involve talking about unwritten rules if you get them 'wrong'. One key example of this is where a neurodivergent person slips up in relation to the hierarchy and treats a senior manager with less respect than expected. This is a situation where advocacy is very important as a mistake can result in disciplinary action.

- The work itself isn't suitable. Sometimes the work allocated is not suitable or appropriate. Advocacy can involve explaining to your manager why the work is unsuitable and why you are going to struggle with it. This can be a really difficult thing to do but being given suitable work is going to benefit everyone.
- Interviews. Job interviews are a huge challenge for many neurodivergent – and particularly autistic – people. Qualified autistics are denied jobs again and again due to challenges with interviews. A job interview favours confident extroverts who are comfortable selling themselves, and these are qualities autistic people tend not to have. Advocacy in this space can involve explaining your needs to interview panels, such as requesting that only one panel member asks the questions or explaining that you do not like eye contact but that doesn't mean you aren't paying attention if you aren't looking at someone.
- Anxiety impacting performance. Anxiety is a big issue in the workplace, and you may be very stressed about work, be that your relationships with managers and colleagues or the work itself and things like deadlines. Others in the workplace will probably have no idea of how anxious you are unless you tell them. While this is challenging, it can in fact feel quite liberating to share your concern. It is important to make sure you tell someone you trust about your anxiety though as some people view mental health issues as a weakness.
- Perfectionism affecting performance. Perfectionism is a form of anxiety and is very common for neurodivergent people in the workplace. Fear of making a mistake can be paralysing and mean you avoid certain tasks. Advocacy around this is often advocacy within yourself. The best strategy for perfectionism is perspective. Ask yourself, 'What will really happen if this goes wrong?' It is often the case that the only person who even noticed a mistake is you and others are totally unaware. Remind yourself that everyone makes mistakes and that they are an opportunity for growth and learning.
- Sexual harassment. Sexual harassment is illegal, but it still happens. It can make work extremely traumatizing and stressful. People feel trapped as they need to go to work to earn money but when they are at work they are being victimized. Sexual

harassment is totally, one hundred per cent the fault of the person doing the harassing. There are strategies for addressing sexual harassment which involve talking to the HR department in your workplace – if you have one – telling the perpetrator's manager or talking to the union, if you are a member of one.

CHAPTER 3

Managing Issues in the Workplace

Gut feelings

A times, we may experience an odd feeling and we can't quite place why we are feeling it. We know that something is up, but don't know what is causing it. When we take the time to sit with the feeling, and analyse the current situation in the workplace, we can start to put together what may be affecting us in this way.

It may be that you have been asked to do a task but the way it was conveyed to you didn't sound quite right. There was a change in the tone of the person who said it to you. Picking up on these subtle cues can be essential in working out how you are feeling. Many neurodivergent people are also highly empathic and sense the feelings of other people around them quite strongly. Another person may not pick up these slight changes in tone, but to neurodivergent people, it triggers a response telling them that something is not quite right.

When you act on these feelings, you are attempting to resolve the uncertainty. If you don't act on these feelings, they can build into anxiety and stress and after a few hours or days you can't figure out why you are feeling so anxious as nothing obvious has immediately happened that you can identify. Those subtle feelings can get suppressed or lost during the day, but they do stay with you, adding to mental stress.

What you can do in situations like this is act immediately. If the person is sounding indifferent, then ask them if they are feeling okay. Often it only takes something small, like asking if the person is okay, to find a solution. If you are sensing hostility, anger or irritability in the tone, you can ask the person if there is a problem with this job as they seem somewhat tense. Is there anything you can do to help here? If you don't feel safe in asking the person, speak to a colleague, supervisor or employer to see if there is anything wrong and anything you can do. By asking, you are seeking clarity which can reduce your internal feelings.

Sometimes the answers you get may seem quite negative, but all communication creates a starting point to resolve a situation. The sooner you can identify the problem, the sooner you can put your anxiety and stress to rest.

Toxicity in the workplace

When a colleague or supervisor is being angry or hostile towards you, you need to consider if this person or people or the whole environment is making the workplace toxic. If you are being treated poorly, you need to address the situation. Talk to other work colleagues, to supervisors and to your employer about the situation and what is actually happening.

If your manager or employer fails to respond or act accordingly, you do have rights. Having a good understanding of the workplace and policy procedures, and familiarizing yourself with these and your rights, will help you in taking the correct action when the workplace is toxic and you can't see a way to resolve the situation.

You can look at seeking mediation from an outside source to help you with the particular situation if you are not getting any support in the workplace. You can ask a colleague you trust to support you in mediation meetings to help you feel validated if you are being gaslighted or manipulated.

Another thing to consider is whether your sense of worth and value is being eroded due to the toxic environment in the workplace. Is this job really for you, do you need to change jobs, if you're able to do that, and if so, what course of action should you take next? Staying in a toxic environment is detrimental to your well-being and mental health. There is no way around this and no matter how hard you try to make the workplace better and less toxic, if the workplace is not prepared to take action and change then you are essentially causing yourself more stress.

Good self-determination and self-advocacy is to find a resolution or leave. No one deserves to have their sense of self, well-being, confidence and value eroded through a toxic working environment. When you put things into perspective, if you get out of the toxic environment, you are looking after yourself. You may experience financial struggles due to this, but if you plan well, you can manage and get by until you find a workplace that will value you, support you and help you thrive.

Also remember, you are not a failure when you leave a toxic environment. You are looking out for yourself; you are taking a stand against what is bad for you and encouraging other colleagues not to put up with toxic working conditions. You are taking control of the standards you want and deserve in order to be respected.

Bullying and toxic people

Another issue with toxic workplaces is bullying and harassment. This sort of behaviour can be quite obvious, but it can also be quite subtle, and people may think you are misinterpreting the situation. This is where your gut feelings help you in understanding the situation and identifying if a person is being unpleasant or is manipulating you, rather than you feeling as if you are misunderstanding the situation.

Manipulation and gaslighting

An example of manipulation is dreading going to work because you don't know what to expect from the employer or work colleague. Half the time they appear friendly, supportive and a great mentor, but at other times they can be a completely different person. They can offer to help you out but then make you feel obligated to do something for them. You may entrust the person with sensitive information and then find they have used it against you or confided in other people about you, which is a great violation of trust.

Other situations can make you feel afraid to share your thoughts or ideas in case of a backlash or being made to feel small. You may do work for a colleague with the idea that you are helping them out, only to find they have taken all the credit for the work.

Often, neurodivergent people will not recognize these signs of manipulation until it is too late. We easily trust people, expecting that they will treat us the same way we treat them. These manipulators are often out to use people to build their career, to boost their ego or to control people around them. They feel empowered by having control in the situation, taking the advantage and leaving the other person demoralized. You may not experience these feelings at first, but over time and with reflection, you will find that the patterns become obvious.

The manipulator is controlling your behaviour and decisions to get what they want, and derailing your success in the workplace by making you feel less than them.

Signs that you are being manipulated

You feel depressed, fearful, anxious or sad around this person

As previously discussed with gut feelings, you may have a slight sense that something is not quite right, disregarding the anxious feelings as nothing and continuing to concede to the needs and demands of the manipulator. It is not until some time later, once your self-esteem and self-worth have been eroded, that the realization hits that you have been manipulated. You feel it is now too late to get out of the situation and are fearful to say no to this person, and this sends you into depression because you don't know how to get away from the toxic situation.

You feel obligated

Obligation can be a form of manipulation, especially when the manipulator expects something in return from you, even if it makes you uncomfortable. What is worse, if you do not fulfil your obligation to this person, they have an uncanny way of making you feel guilty, even if you disagree with what they are asking of you, and you know it is wrong.

You change your behaviour/morals to suit the manipulator

In manipulating relationships, the person being manipulated will often change their behaviour, their moral standing and approach to work in an attempt to please the manipulator. Unfortunately, no matter how much you change to try and please the manipulator, they are never going to be satisfied. Their energy is gained by controlling you and making you feel less than them. All you will do is expend your energy and feel drained and defeated around this type of person. They are energy thieves.

The manipulator's behaviour/reactions are unpredictable

This is where it becomes difficult in the early days of recognizing if the person is using you or is a genuinely supportive colleague. Often in the beginning, they can appear helpful, friendly and on your side, then pow, their behaviour suddenly changes, and you ask yourself, where on earth did that come from? You will question yourself as to what you did wrong, or maybe you missed something, leading to you becoming anxious and stressed over why the other person is angry and upset.

Usually, you have done nothing wrong. It can be due to something totally unrelated, but they will take it out on you and there is nothing you can do to prevent or stop this behaviour as it is always completely unexpected, unwanted and unacceptable.

You feel your sense of value is being lost

A manipulator will find a way to make you feel devalued. They may call you awful things that insult your intelligence. They will point out that your ideas are ridiculous or that your opinion is not wanted. They will also downplay your achievements. They may say that anyone could do that thing, that you didn't deserve the recognition, and question what all the fuss is about.

Another subtle way a manipulator can devalue you is by not actively listening to you. As we know, many autistics and neurodivergent people dislike eye contact. This is very different from the lack of eye contact from a manipulator. When the manipulator is not looking at you or actively engaging with you, they are devaluing you.

Barb has experienced this at events where there are a variety of people from different organizations attending. Sometimes, the person she was with would not actively listen to what she was saying, instead scouting the room to look for more important or prominent people they could talk to, to inflate their sense of self-importance. This sort of behaviour leaves you feeling diminished, inadequate and that you are not important enough to be there.

How do we stop manipulation?

Prevention is always the best approach, but this can be difficult as often we don't recognize we are being manipulated until it is too late. It is important to learn how to identify what you are feeling and connect it to the situation. Ask colleagues or supervisors or employers if they feel there is something not quite right with the person of concern or if they are experiencing problems with them. If the person has been in the workplace for a while, you can guarantee you are not their first victim and there will be others who have experienced this manipulation.

You need to establish strong boundaries, even if the person makes you feel uncomfortable. You are doing this for your own well-being, and making a statement that you will not tolerate this type of behaviour and manipulation. Often, once the person has been rejected and strong boundaries are in place, they will back off and look for someone else who will give in to their requests. This is where it is useful to speak with employers or management to highlight the problematic person, so that more action can be taken to ensure other employees are not subjected to this type of behaviour.

If you feel you are being manipulated, document each action and interaction you have with the person. Write down how you are feeling, what is being asked of you and how they behaved. By doing this you are creating clarity about the problematic behaviour that you are experiencing and it is incredibly helpful when making a complaint about the person to management.

By standing up for your worth and values and setting strong boundaries, you are taking care of your mental well-being, as well as being part of the change in a toxic workplace.

CHAPTER 4

Managing Issues in Relationships

Relationships come in many forms. These can be friendships, romantic and intimate relationships, and relationships that are part of our everyday lives when we are at work with bosses and colleagues or in an educational setting at school or university. Common to all these relationships is that there is usually more than one person involved and they require navigation of hidden expectations and the dynamics of interaction and connection with other people. It is within these relationships that we need to have good self-determination skills to identify what we want and be able to speak out if we feel uncomfortable or that the relationship is not good for us or is toxic or unsafe.

Intimate relationships

Being in a romantic relationship usually involves two people who are intimate with each other, usually sexually, and make a commitment to each other and do everything possible to make the relationship work. This commitment is the underlying glue and foundation for having a good relationship and is what turns romance into real love.

However, some relationships can involve more than two people when it is done on an open and accepting basis, and an intimate relationship does not have to include sexual activities. This is determined by your desires and needs as well as considering the other person's needs.

Key components of typical intimate relationships include:

- Intimacy – the emotional component of your relationship. This is when you can relax and be your true self around another person, sharing your innermost thoughts and feelings, trusting the other, knowing that they will consistently be supportive of you and will keep your secrets without betraying you.
- Passion – the physical component of your relationship. This is the desire to touch, kiss, hold, make love and so on.
- Commitment – the intellectual component of the relationship. When problems arise, you work through them, and you stay together, no matter what.

Types of intimate relationships

- Physical. This may include being inside someone's personal space, holding hands, cuddling, kissing, intimate touching or sexualized activities and sex.
- Emotional. This develops after trust and personal bonds have been established. This can evolve from sexual relationships. The emotional connection of falling in love comes from sexual or intellectual attraction and social connection through talking.
- Cognitive or intellectual intimacy. This occurs when two people share ideas and enjoy intellectual dialogue about their similarities on a topic they are both interested in and discussions that have different views and opinions that grow their knowledge base.
- Spiritual. This type of relationship forms by having a spiritual connection with another person. This can be due to similarities in faith or experiencing a sense of transcendence through bonding.

Physical sensations

This involves a lot of sensory experiences. Many autistic people have a variety of sensory issues that can be amplified during physical contact. Some autistic people don't like to be hugged. But why is this? It can be due to the fact they don't like the type of sensation when they are being hugged, or they might only like really firm hugs or prefer to be hugged for a very limited amount of time due to becoming overwhelmed with sensory overload. For example, Barb dislikes people giving her light touches or hugs as they make her skin crawl and feel hypersensitive. It feels as if she has an allergy and wants to start scratching her skin as it is annoying. If you wipe away a wisp of hair from her face as a sign of affection, you are more likely to get a swat from her and a not-so-loving response in return!

Many autistic people like to be asked before being touched or hugged as they need a moment to prepare for the incoming sensation. Also, if they are overwhelmed already, they may not want someone hugging or touching them at all, so not respecting the person's needs of not wanting to be touched can lead to negative outcomes and further shutdown. If they say, 'Don't touch me', it means exactly that. Neurotypical or neurodivergent people should not force themselves on you and this also goes for children too. If great-aunty wants a kiss and the child is thinking, 'Not on your life', the child's wishes need to be respected. It can be traumatic.

This goes for any type of intimate or sexual touching. As with every relationship, we need to be respectful of the other person's needs. Some may dislike the feeling of bodily fluids and instead of being part of the positive intimate experience, it can lead to feelings of nausea and aversion. A good visual example is that of eggs that are not quite cooked. The white of the egg is not quite done and has that jelly consistency, which can make you feel sick and as if you don't want to eat any of the egg at all. In sexual relationships, this can also be the response to seeing or touching bodily fluids.

Smells and odours

This one is pretty obvious to all of us. When your partner is all stinky from sweating and working all day and wants to give you a hug, the first thing you want to do is run or swat them off you. Now this can happen when we are super clean too. Perfumes, scents and even naturally added scents like lavender or orange can create a similar response. Often many of these smells are chemically based and when an autistic person has hypersensitivities to smell, they can be problematic.

Your partner may have scrubbed themselves up with scented body wash, applied scented deodorant and put on their best aftershave ready for an intimate night in, only to find themselves sleeping alone while you sleep in the spare room with a box of tissues and popping antihistamines.

It's the same with not washing enough and not brushing teeth.

You need to tell your partner clearly what your aversions and likes are so they can respect what is good for you. A good compromise can be using non-scented deodorant that does the job of getting rid of the body odours but also removes the risks of sensory overwhelm from highly perfumed products.

Sounds and noises

As with any relationship, there will be bodily noises of all kinds that can occur. If you are someone like Barb who has misophonia (a severe sensitivity to specific soft sounds and visual images), certain noises can feel like road-rage for the ears. When she hears a person eating within close proximity, the slurping, crushing, smacking, masticating sounds immediately ignite the music from the movie *Psycho*, and she gets this burning rage of wanting to do something unpleasant to them. Apparently, this response is connected to our flight or fight response and is triggered in the brain, not by our ears (Kumar *et al.*, 2017). If you take a look at the different response Barb has to sounds such as dogs licking themselves, where she wants to vomit and run away, it makes sense as to why one response triggers fight and the other flight. There is still very little research on this condition.

So, you can see how this would really dampen the mood when having a nice romantic dinner. It could be a recipe for disaster. How do you have a romantic dinner without your partner running out the door or threatening to stab you with a fork?

With some careful consideration and understanding of your own and your partner's sensory profile, you can usually find ways to do these things. For example, your partner might love heavy metal music, so a romantic dinner for them could be scoffing a burger while watching the local metal band that is deafening the whole street. You certainly won't hear anyone eating! If you have misophonia, you can reduce the annoying sounds by wearing ear buds that allow you to still hear conversation, or, instead of eating without conversation, ignite a robust discussion about saving the planet or politics – that would distract anyone's attention long enough to consume the food.

Now, let's take these sounds to the bedroom... You remember the sensation of hearing dogs licking themselves, well there can be lots of squishing, licking – you get the drift – bedroom noises that could cause the same reaction. This needs really careful consideration as to how to overcome the noises and it may mean that while you are making out, you need to play something like Prince's '1999' turned up to level 10 and set on repeat. But be careful you don't upset the neighbours. Having them knock on your window mid-passion is certainly a mood killer.

Is sex important?

This is completely dependent on the type of relationship you want. You can have a relationship without sex. Intellect can be just as satisfying – for example, talking about quantum physics may give you an intellectual orgasm.

Remember, you are the master of your body. There must always be consent. There are no restrictions on what a healthy sexual diet is as long as you are not causing harm, distress or pressuring the other person. If both parties are consenting, then it is up to you what makes you feel good.

Sex can be an intense interest – you could know more positions than the *Kama Sutra*!

Pornography

Pornography can be a satisfying and pleasurable experience when considered in a healthy and respectful manner. Here are some things to think about if you are contemplating watching pornography by yourself or with your partner:

- What is classified safe? For example, is the content showing people in healthy and realistic sexual relationships?

- What is considered an addiction? How often do you or your partner watch pornography and is it impacting on your relationship?
- Are you or your partner hiding your viewing or excluding the other person from viewing?
- Is there a danger of preferring porn over real-life sex?
- Do you or your partner have unrealistic idealization – expecting the other to perform acts like a porn star?
- Does the porn sex inflict violence, rape and degradation?
- Is the content promoting child pornography?

Where possible, always openly talk with your partner about porn, what you both consider as pleasurable, and always be firm in conveying your personal values, ideals and morals if you feel uncomfortable when being asked to watch something that you do not agree with. It is never okay to sit through watching something to just make your partner feel good. Everyone should feel okay with what they are experiencing.

Sexuality

When you learn more about what you like in terms of intimate relationships, the better you will become at advocating for what you want and do not want. When you know yourself, it can:

- help in understanding who you are
- give clarity as to why you do things the way you do
- help you learn about your sensory profile
- enable you to stop pretending to be someone you are not
- finally grow into the person you want to be.

Some things to consider with intimate relationships:

- Every relationship is different.
- There are no set rules.
- Communication is the key to success.

Living together

Things to ponder when considering living with someone:

- How long have you known them? Do you need more time to get to know them better before moving in together?
- Do they do things that make you cringe? How will you feel when living together if they continue to do these things? How will you tell them that you do not like what they do?
- Will you be able to do what you want to do after you move in together? If you have to give up things that you enjoy to be in a relationship, it may be worth considering if this the right relationship for you.
- Are you prepared to compromise? There will always be a need to compromise as each person will not get everything they want.
- Have you considered the financial aspect of living together? How will you plan who will pay for what?

You can have relationships without living together. Many of us like our own space, and we often like time alone or prefer to only spend a short amount of time with someone. If you don't live together, you are free to design your home the way that suits you and is accommodating to you. You don't have to live with someone to be in a relationship.

Having children

This is your choice alone. Do not be pressured into having children if you do not want to, as it is perfectly fine not to have children. But if you want children, have them! Autistic parents are awesome! Or if you want to just have cats (or dogs), that is perfectly fine too!

Personal safety

What to expect in dating and relationships and how to be assertive when not comfortable with the situation:

- Recognize dangerous situations – for example, being alone with another person you have only just met, and they are making unwanted advances towards you.
- Be wary of drink spiking. When going out in social situations with lots of people you do not know, for example to a pub or nightclub, make sure to keep your drink within your sight and never leave it with people you do not know. Have a trusted friend to look out for you.

Emotional abuse

Emotional abuse in relationships can look like:

- unequal workloads
- broken promises
- isolating you from friends and family
- humiliation
- gaslighting
- narcissist behaviour
- disrespect for you
- criticism of your looks or intelligence.

Issues with partners

This is a difficult area for advocacy as it is quite personal and issues tend to be specific to individuals but there are elements of relationships where advocacy is beneficial:

- Assumptions about neurodivergence. A partner who makes assumptions about their neurodivergent partner, particularly negative assumptions, can be called out on this. Assumptions do not form a positive basis for a relationship so if it is happening in your relationship it is beneficial to address it. This can be done by giving examples of neurodivergent people – or you – who are not living out the stereotype. Introducing your partner to other neurodivergent people can help.

- Controlling behaviour. Some partners are controlling. This is not okay. If they are controlling without realizing they are being so, there is some opportunity to raise this with them; but if it is conscious and intentional then that is a significant problem. It is better to leave a relationship with an intentionally controlling partner. One way you can discover if your partner is being intentionally controlling or not is to call them out on it. It can help to write down your concerns and show your partner this. If they respond apologetically or say that they intend to change based on your advice, then it indicates that your relationship is a probably good thing. If they respond with anger and more controlling behaviour then it may indicate that the relationship is not worth keeping. Please note that they may respond with anger initially and then come to the realization that their behaviour is controlling.
- Ableism. Sometimes partners may be ableist. This can be evidenced by their language or behaviour. If your partner uses ableist language and insults, it is a space for advocacy. You can call them out on this and explain how it makes you feel when they do it. Ableism can be quite ingrained and many people are ableist without even knowing it.
- Domestic and family violence. If you are in an abusive relationship and you can leave, then leave. Domestic violence happens a lot and more often for disabled people, usually women. Violence and abuse does not have to involve physical violence. It can include gaslighting, emotional abuse and controlling behaviour. Perpetrators of domestic violence may seem sweet and charming at first. They may also apologize for being abusive and perform gestures in apology (such as buying flowers for the victim). However, do not be fooled by this. It is part of the abuse.
- People in domestic violence situations need support, especially if they choose to leave the relationship. Perpetrators of domestic violence can be extremely dangerous, and attempted murders frequently happen in these situations. This is not something you can manage alone. There are services in many countries to support people fleeing domestic violence. If you have a trusted friend or family member, tell them what is happening. You can also talk to a disability support organization. It is important to

have support, and to let people who can help know what is happening.

CHAPTER 5

Advocacy in Old Age

Having good self-advocacy skills as we age is just as critical as it is in the first years of our life. As we age, we often find we are in more need of visits to medical professionals, hospitals and therapists, along with support in the home or in residential care settings.

We need to be able to ask for clarification, especially when health professionals are providing therapy, minor surgery or medication. This is also applicable in hospital and emergency environments. We need to be able to speak up and ask for clarification of what is happening to us, as quite often when we don't say anything, the medical professionals won't give us any extra information or details, or if they do, we may forget everything they have said to us, leaving us feeling confused or frustrated.

Health professionals may also use technical language which often many people do not understand. We have the right to ask for an explanation in simple language that will help us understand what we are taking in terms of medication, what the reactions might be, how it can improve our well-being and what the expectations and outcomes of using this medication are. Being able to self-advocate and ask for this clarification also helps to reduce unnecessary anxiety and stress from not having all the information.

If you're feeling rushed, for example in a doctor's office, you can ask the doctor to write down the terms you are not familiar with, which you can take out to the administrative staff on your way out or while you are booking another appointment and ask for further clarification, as they often have a lot of knowledge in these areas. Ask if they can provide you with fact sheets so you can learn more information as well. Also ask if they can provide you with information hotlines which can also help you with medical advice.

Be prepared prior to going to your appointment. Have a list of what you want to ask and have key words that may trigger you to ask for more information when unsure. Your notes could also consist of a quick self-check-in. For example, when the doctor asks you if there is anything else, take a look at your list and tune in to how you feel. If you are feeling anxious, ask yourself why. This should provide you with the question you need to ask the doctor. It could be that you are feeling anxious about having to go and get an xray. You could ask the doctor for more information on the process or ask the administrative staff after the appointment. Knowing yourself and how you feel can help you to ask for more information and support.

If you require the support of a carer, you can give them valuable information about yourself that will help them organize when you need to take medication or when you need to make another appointment, or have them go through the details with you so that you understand better what is expected or what will happen to you.

In hospital situations, it can become very overwhelming as there are so many people and often different people due to the regular changes of shifts. In this situation, make a note prior to hospital admission of your needs and concerns, and if you have sensory concerns, you can convey these on admission. Ideally do this in a written format where you can provide a list of your supports and print out multiple copies that you can hand out where you think it is needed. You can also keep these with you and give them to nurses or doctors to help them quickly ascertain that you may need extra support and further clarification, or if you struggle, for example, with being touched by different people.

Self-advocacy is also important if you are not happy with the medical care of doctors or providers that are looking after you, and you wish to make a change from the person treating you. Understanding that you have rights to be treated well will help you in determining whether you wish to persist with the current support or change to another person. Often, you will find there are rules and regulations that support your choice of discontinuing or changing service providers.

In Australia, this is quite clear under the National Disability Insurance Scheme, where providers delivering a service should have a service agreement in place outlining the expectations of what will happen when a participant wishes to no longer use their services or change to another provider. Again, we can see here that knowing and learning what your rights are will help you in advocating and conveying your choices.

Aged care facilities

Some people need to move to an aged care facility. This can be challenging for neurotypical people but particularly so for neurodivergent people. Advocacy is a necessary element of moving into an aged care home. It can be difficult to convey your needs to staff. It can help to enlist a trusted family member or friend to co-advocate with you. It can be very challenging advocating for yourself in this situation as it can be overwhelming and stressful. Issues you might encounter in an aged care facility include sensory problems, being close to neighbours or having to share a room. Being clear about your needs and explaining that you are neurodivergent and what that means for you in the context of the aged care facility is a good approach. You may need to continue your advocacy with staff after you move in.

Wills

The one constant in life is that everyone dies. A lot of us don't want to think about death but it is inevitable and being prepared makes it easier for those we leave behind.

Part of being prepared for death is making a will. Everyone should have a legal will, not just older people. This is particularly true if you have assets (home, superannuation, savings etc.). You can get a will drawn up by a solicitor. There is a cost, but it is usually a one-off expense. Give consideration to who you want to leave things to in your will. You will also need to appoint an executor, who will:

- contact the beneficiaries in the will and notify them of their entitlements
- value the estate and then keep records of the valuations
- make financial decisions based on the assets and money in your estate
- organize the payment of any debts

- liaise with the Tax Office and complete any outstanding income tax returns
- divide the estate, and supply relevant documentation to all beneficiaries.

The executor is a responsible position so choose someone you trust and who you think is capable of the task.

Planning for your funeral

Another part of being prepared for death is planning for your funeral. You can take out funeral insurance which covers most or all of the costs of your funeral. You can also tell a trusted person about your plans for your funeral. What kind of service do you want? Do you want to be buried or cremated? What music do you want played at the service? Some funeral homes allow you to prearrange your funeral when you are still alive. It can be stressful talking about your death and you might feel overwhelmed. As such, it pays to be prepared for conversations about your funeral. You can write down things you want to say in conversations about your funeral, and questions you want to ask.

CHAPTER 6

Advocacy in Different Settings, Including Healthcare

Civic life

Everyone has the right to take part in civic life (e.g. politics, clubs, interest groups). Sometimes, neurodivergent people are discouraged from participating and treated as if they have nothing to contribute. Advocacy in this space can include putting yourself forward as a candidate for governance of clubs and interest groups, active participation in committees and boards, taking responsibility in clubs, and even standing for election to government.

Having and expressing opinions about politics is a right. While not everyone has an interest in politics, for those neurodivergent people that do it is important that they are supported to be heard and respected. Neurodivergent people have exactly the same rights to a political opinion and to participate in elections and political life as anyone else does. It is an immensely ableist view that says neurodivergent people shouldn't participate in politics, political discussions or elections. Advocacy in this space can involve opening a conversation around the value of engagement in politics by all members of society.

Advocacy in the neurodivergent community

It can be said that part of the neurodivergent community is those with an interest in neurodivergence, such as allistic parents of autistic kids.

Some of these people are genuine allies but some are problematic and want to make the conversation all about them. This can be quite daunting and invalidating for neurodivergent people. It is an area requiring advocacy. Some allistic people try to advocate on behalf of neurodivergent people but instead of advocacy what happens is erasure and silencing of neurodivergent voices.

It can be hard to counter such silencing, especially if the person doing the talking is someone you love and respect, such as one of your parents. Advocacy in this space can be very challenging. It is worth approaching a neurodivergent friend or a genuine ally to help address the issue and convey a supportive message. Recognize that this is a huge problem for neurodivergent people, with certain large organizations (such as Autism Speaks) specializing in counteracting this kind of invalidating behaviour. The weight of ableist history may seem to support exclusionary views and things being done without consultation of neurodivergent people but it is possible to fight against that history with an inclusive message. This is not something you can do alone. The neurodivergent community has a lot of advocates in it working together to address that history. It is a matter of working together and aligning ourselves to fight ableism and people speaking for us without our consent.

Accessing healthcare

Accessing healthcare can be an extremely fraught area for neurodivergent people. Clinicians can have outdated attitudes or little or no knowledge about neurodivergent conditions – and neurodivergent people. Many neurodivergent people avoid seeking any help for health matters at all, following negative experiences. Healthcare can be unhelpful, damaging or even dangerous and many would rather suffer in silence than try to access assistance.

Finding a good clinician can sometimes be almost impossible, and good clinicians can leave or retire, resulting in a stressful search for a new health professional who will help rather than hinder. It can pay to talk to other neurodivergent people about which clinicians are helpful – either close friends or people in online and other support groups.

You can even put together a list of useful and supportive clinicians and share this within your networks.

General practitioners (GPs)

Having an approachable, professional and supportive GP who 'gets' you is essential. They are your first port of call for health check-ups and regular tests to ensure you stay healthy, and can refer you to other clinicians and specialists. Having a good relationship with your GP is therefore really important. Some clinicians can be educated and trained to be more helpful. While some doctors are arrogant and won't listen to a patient, others are keen to improve their performance and increase their knowledge. In this situation, advocacy is a really useful strategy. You can explain to your doctor about your needs and how you experience the world. Not only will this benefit you, but it will also benefit any other neurodivergent individuals who use your doctor. It is okay to change doctors as well. You do not have to stay with the same one if you don't want to, especially if they are being unhelpful or they don't listen to you.

Hospital

Going to hospital can be extremely stressful and unpleasant for neurodivergent people. Bright lights, noise, people coming and going, uncertainty about what will happen next, confusion about what is happening and concerns about a loved one's health can conspire to make it a very unpleasant experience. Hospital staff might have a poor understanding of neurodivergence. They may mean well but have very little understanding and, in some cases, they are actively hostile. Things like meltdowns or sensory overload can be viewed by hospital staff as poor behaviour or aggression, leading to unhelpful treatment. Even if you tell staff that you are neurodivergent, they may not know what that means for you.

For these reasons, some neurodivergent people avoid going to hospital even if they need to go. If you are too unwell or too overloaded to advocate for yourself in hospital, it can help to have a family member, friend or your partner advocating for you. It can help to make a document listing your needs and triggers for overload to give to hospital staff if necessary. This document can list what will make you overloaded, what hospital staff can do to help you de-escalate and feel more comfortable, who to call if you are in hospital and other information you feel it is useful for staff to know.

It can help to have someone stay with you when you are in hospital. If you don't have a friend, partner or family member to do this and you are feeling overloaded and you think this would help, ask the hospital to provide an assistant in nursing to stay with you when you are there. When asking for this you can explain how being in hospital impacts on you and that you are at risk of overload/meltdown without that support.

Being in hospital – as a patient or a visitor – can be extremely traumatic for neurodivergent people and can result in high levels of stress as well as being invalidated and not heard by staff.

This article by Yenn Purkis (2016) from *The Mighty* demonstrates some of the issues autistic people have in emergency room settings:

> I'm autistic and also have a mental illness. I've had to go emergency rooms in hospitals a number of times. The experience has always been traumatic and unhelpful. I've experienced a lot of paternalism, been treated as if I'm a naughty child and invalidated in many other ways.
>
> In some cases, these experiences have resulted in me avoiding seeking treatment for mental and physical health complaints, which in fact did require urgent treatment.
>
> Autistic people – both patients and visitors – will be anxious and scared in the emergency room. Sometimes autistic people will be unable to speak or clearly express what they're experiencing.
>
> Here are 10 things that could help ER staffers to assist autistic patients, visitors and support people:
>
> 1. Don't assume autistic patients and visitors are being deliberately difficult. Autistic communication tends to be different from non-autistic communication, and can lead to misunderstandings, even when the autistic person isn't in a highly

stressful situation like accessing emergency health care. If we seem difficult, please do not assume we mean to be.

2. After their medical status is confirmed as not requiring immediate emergency intervention, ask the autistic person what they need, what they think would help and how you can assist. If their requests can't be accommodated, explain this to them and the reasons why. Some people may prefer to communicate via typing or facilitated communicate device, rather than verbal communication. If this is the case, find a way to accommodate their needs.

3. For autistic people, emotional, sensory and/or information overload can lead to a meltdown. The ER is often an overwhelming place. It has people coming and going, often with visible injuries, odd smells, glaring lights and confusing information. Being unwell enough to be present at the ER and having a meltdown is unpleasant for the autistic person and possibly other people in the ER who might be frightened.

   The overload which leads to a meltdown can be addressed by decreasing the stimuli causing it. Often this can involve simple measures like explaining what's going on as well as you can and providing a quiet space.

   If someone does have a meltdown, trying to intervene will almost certainly exacerbate it. Leave the person alone. If you have to say something, stand back from the person and offer supportive, calm comments. Do not try to physically restrain the person or tell them off for their 'poor behavior'. A meltdown is not poor behavior or a way to seek attention – it's a response to overload.

4. Waiting for an indeterminate amount of time is stressful to almost all autistic people and any relatives with them. If an autistic person asks you how long they will wait for treatment or to be taken to a bed in the ward once the decision to admit the patient is made, they aren't being difficult or pushy, they're just anxious because they want to understand how long they will be there for.

   Respond as accurately as you can. Even a little bit of information such as, 'We are quite busy tonight, so it may be a few hours', is more helpful than no information. This

information is also useful to relatives waiting with the patient. They may choose to get some food or go home and
sleep if it'll be a long wait.

5. Some autistic people don't have family, a partner or friend to
   support them and may attend the ER alone. Consider what
   they may be going through: They're unwell enough to seek
   help in a hospital, which is probably not a place they would
   choose to attend otherwise. They're in a situation that can be
   triggering, unfamiliar and scary. A staff member periodically
   coming up and asking them briefly if they're OK or offering
   a hot drink can make a huge difference. This doesn't need
   to be time consuming,

6. Many autistic people experience sensory issues and overload.
   Bright lights may be overwhelming, and unfamiliar smells,
   medical equipment making unexpected noises and under-
   going uncomfortable medical procedures administered by
   strangers can be quite traumatic. Consider making some of
   the waiting room space and beds on the ward sensory friendly.
   This doesn't need to be onerous and can simply involve using
   incandescent lighting in an area of the waiting room, screen-
   ing off an area and providing fidget or sensory toys.

7. Medical staff should explain as clearly as possible to autistic
   patients what is happening. If possible, provide the likely
   duration for results of medical tests being returned. It's
   OK to qualify these statements by saying the time may vary,
   but having some kind of ballpark timeframe and reason for
   medical tests and procedures can reduce anxiety.

8. Autistic family and friends may be highly anxious about the
   person they're supporting. Some practical measures to assist
   autistic friends and family of patients are quiet areas in the
   waiting room, somewhere to buy food since many autistic
   people are sensitive to being hungry, which can trigger stress
   or meltdowns, being given approximate waiting times and
   being told what's happening as much as possible.

9. It may help to develop a tip sheet to provide to autistic
   patients and visitors, which includes information on the
   triage process, how to access assistance if overloaded, what
   the expected behaviours are in the ER, where to access Wi-Fi

or charging points for devices and where to go to provide feedback or complaints. Staff training around autism can also be very helpful.

10. Consider having a supply of cheap items to reduce sensory overload available in the ER for patients and support people who need them: ear plugs, sleep masks (especially for those in ER overnight) and a small number of fidget toys.

Waiting for indefinite periods, physically invasive procedures, probing questions, sensory triggers and patronizing or downright hostile staff are just a few of the issues neurodivergent people can come across when in hospital.

In terms of advocacy, it is wise to have a support person with you in hospital. It also pays to be aware of your medical condition(s) if possible and to have knowledge of any medications you are taking. Be aware that hospital is likely to be a very unpleasant experience and that you – or your support person – will probably need to stand up for yourself at least once.

When advocating in a hospital setting there are a few strategies that can help:

- If something a staff member says or does seems wrong, question it.
- Ask about medications, particularly new medication – what is it for, what are the potential side effects, does it interact negatively with medication you are currently taking?
- If you need something – such as sensory accommodations, or a warm blanket – say something to the nurse or nursing assistant looking after you.
- If you are getting overloaded and it is possible to do so, say something.
- Tell staff what your neurodivergence means to you, what your triggers for overload are and what your specific needs are.
- If you have a chronic condition, especially a mental health condition, consider making an advance agreement listing critical information for your care to provide to hospital staff.
- If you are discriminated against, you can make a formal complaint.

Your experience in hospital and particularly your interaction with the staff will impact on their thoughts about other neurodivergent people. You can help change the experience others have by your advocacy. You might not feel like this when you are feeling unwell and helpless but it is a comforting thought nevertheless.

Accessing mental health care

Accessing mental health care can be particularly fraught for neurodivergent people. There are a lot of assumptions which mental health clinicians can have around neurodivergent people. There is also a lot of ignorance and stereotyping. Accessing support for mental health issues can be extremely hard and can exacerbate the symptoms of mental health conditions.

Example: Autism and borderline personality disorder

Autistic people – and especially autistic women – are frequently misdiagnosed with a condition called borderline personality disorder. This is negative for a range of reasons, mostly because it is hard to access appropriate support when you have a misdiagnosis but also because in the mental health field, people with borderline personality disorder suffer prejudice and discrimination and are often viewed as being manipulative and attention-seeking.

There are real reasons for this frequent misdiagnosis. Elements of autism can look like elements of borderline personality disorder. Autistic people often have issues with alexithymia (being able to identify their emotions), meaning that they can go from zero to 100 very quickly emotions-wise. This looks like something called emotion dysregulation in borderline personality disorder. Another similarity between the two is that autistic women can mask their symptoms or adapt to their situation, meaning that their identity can appear to change. This changing of identity to fit the situation is also part of borderline personality disorder. Another similarity is self-harming – something autistic people often do and which is also a key part of a borderline personality disorder diagnosis. You can imagine why a clinician with very little understanding of autism would give someone the wrong diagnosis based on all of this. For people given an incorrect diagnosis, this knowledge probably doesn't help much but it does indicate how important it is for clinicians to be educated in treating neurodivergent patients.

Crisis support

Many people with mental health conditions go through mental health crises. This is a time of extreme stress and emotion and can be very dangerous in terms of suicidal thoughts and behaviour. Neurodivergent people can go through meltdowns combined with mental health crises, which is a perfect storm of extreme feelings. The important thing to know about crises is that they are time limited. A crisis usually lasts for less than an hour. It can help to plan some strategies for when a crisis happens and share these with family, friends, partner and also mental health workers.

There are mental health crisis services in many countries. These services are there for when someone experiences a crisis. Some are telephone calling services, and some are online chat services. It is important to know that not all crisis services are helpful and that the quality of the services is largely dependent on the individual counsellor you speak with. Some crisis services are staffed by mental health clinicians and some by volunteers. You do not have to be actively suicidal to call these services. Be aware that some staff on crisis lines are very understanding of neurodivergent people, but some aren't. It is very hard to be assertive when you are experiencing a crisis but if you have a negative experience you can contact the organization which runs the service (mental health clinic/volunteer organization) afterwards and outline that you had a negative experience and what you would prefer to have happened. If you feel unable to do this, ask someone you trust to do so on your behalf. It is not okay for crisis services to be unhelpful and to make matters worse. When you are experiencing a crisis you need support, respect and understanding.

Seeing psychiatrists

Psychiatrists can be very helpful but, unfortunately, they can also be arrogant and damaging. Many psychiatrists have little understanding of neurodiversity and treating neurodivergent patients. Autistic people and those with ADHD can have particular challenges in this area. Psychiatrists can misdiagnose people or prescribe unhelpful and even dangerous medications. Sometimes you will need to change psychiatrists or see a new one in a hospital setting. This can be very anxiety-provoking given the potential for misdiagnoses and medication changes. Many psychiatrists do not listen to their neurodivergent patients so even if you advocate for yourself you may not be heard.

It is possible to get very attached to a good psychiatrist and when they leave or retire, there is the task of locating a new one. This can be very stressful. It can help to take a friend, partner or relative with you to a new psychiatrist appointment or to an appointment with an existing doctor who is being difficult or unhelpful. Another person can act as an advocate and can add an objective presence, as you may find that what is said can be distorted by your anxiety. The person with you at the appointment can also provide evidence if the doctor says or does anything negative. It can also help to write down what you want to get from the appointment and any questions you have for the doctor.

Sometimes you won't have the option to see a different psychiatrist, perhaps if you are in hospital or accessing mental health care through a community clinic. This can make it difficult to advocate for yourself if a psychiatrist behaves inappropriately. However, you still have some recourse, including making a complaint to the hospital/clinic or talking to a community or disability advocacy service. If you see a psychiatrist privately and they behave inappropriately you can simply stop seeing them and find another one. Ask around your neurodivergent peer group (including online) for recommendations of a good psychiatrist in your area. If there are psychiatrists who understand neurodivergence in an area then this is often common knowledge among the local neurodivergent people.

Some people hold a lot of respect for the position of doctor. This can mean they put up with poor treatment from a psychiatrist as they believe the medical opinion is of more value than their own. This is not okay. If a psychiatrist mistreats you or treats you without respect and decency, then they are in the wrong. Everyone deserves respect, including those accessing mental health care. It is not okay for a doctor – or anyone – to disrespect you. Sometimes it pays to ditch some of the attitudes we have inherited from the past. A rule of thumb is that if someone is treating you poorly then they are in the wrong. If you are unsure whether a doctor is treating you poorly, you can ask a trusted friend, family member or your partner. Mistreatment from psychiatrists can be more of a problem for neurodivergent people as we can be quite trusting. If we are decent and respectful, we often assume everyone is, but this is not always the case.

If a psychiatrist mistreats you there are a few courses of action you can take:

- Stop seeing them and find another psychiatrist, if possible.
- Report them to the relevant registration body.
- Speak with them about your concerns and set boundaries for them.
- Speak with a mental health advocacy organization if there is one in your area.

Seeing psychologists

Psychologists can be a very positive addition to your mental health care, but some issues can arise too. Like psychiatrists, psychologists can be arrogant and dismissive. They often focus on one kind of therapy, such as cognitive behavioural therapy (CBT), or acceptance and commitment therapy. There is a perception that CBT is the best therapy model for neurodivergent people but some find CBT unhelpful. You don't want to be arguing with your psychologist about therapy models, so it is best if they have an understanding of your needs.

Talk to you psychologist about your needs, wants and concerns. Remember that you are paying them and they are providing a service, so they are there to support you, not give you a hard time. There can be some issues with psychologists:

- They are inexperienced and don't know what to do to support you.

- They are arrogant and don't listen to you.
- They only use one kind of therapy model and it isn't one that you find helpful.
- They have little or no knowledge of neurodivergence.
- They are bigoted (e.g. racist, transphobic, homophobic) or have unconscious bias against a group you are a member of.

It is important to know what you want to get out of therapy. Do you want to address anxiety, develop some strategies for coping with life, be more able to manage in social situations, or something else? View your psychologist as someone who is there to help you achieve whatever goal you have for your therapy. Remember that you are in charge and you can end the therapeutic relationship if you want to. You can use the strategy of taking a friend, partner or family member into your first or a subsequent session, as suggested with psychiatrists.

CHAPTER 7

Advocacy with Friends and Family Members

Advocacy with friends

Friends can sometimes have problematic attitudes around neurodivergence and may be ableist – either intentionally or with unconscious bias. They may make offensive statements or have attitudes which are unhelpful, saying things such as, 'We are all on the spectrum somewhere.' or, 'You could pass for normal.' It can be more challenging to address this behaviour when it comes from a friend than a stranger or a support person.

Setting boundaries with friends can be very challenging indeed. Assertiveness tends to be harder to achieve when it is a friend that you care about and whose opinions you value and respect.

Advocacy with friends can involve assertiveness and positive boundary setting. Advocacy can involve pulling up a friend if they say something inappropriate about neurodivergence. This can be very difficult, especially if it is a new friend. If the comments are repeated and you feel you cannot speak to the friend directly, it can help to send an email, typed message or letter outlining your concerns. This has the added bonus that you can think about what you are going to say before you say it. It also gives the friend the opportunity to revisit your concerns and consider them before responding to you. The period between the friend seeing the message and responding to you can be anxiety-provoking. Avoid contacting them right away and give them the opportunity to consider what you have said. If they are a friend who values you then they should respond positively.

Some friends are not friends at all and can be toxic and destructive.

Many neurodivergent people are lonely and isolated and take any friendship regardless of whether the 'friend' is actually a friend. These 'friends' can be narcissistic and bullying. They may take advantage of you and exploit you for their entertainment.

The best thing to do with 'friends' like this is not really advocacy, it is boundary setting and will often involve cutting that person from your life. You are better off without these kinds of people in your life. A toxic friendship is not a friendship. While it may seem counterintuitive to break ties with a friend when you don't have a lot of friends in the first place, it is in fact good self-care. When cutting the person from your life you should block them from all your social media, block their phone number and do not respond if they try to contact you. You do not owe this person anything. A toxic 'friend' may:

- be abusive of you, put you down and make you the butt of their jokes
- make you feel unsafe when you are with them
- actively seek out arguments
- have to be right
- be controlling
- be physically aggressive
- lie or be dishonest.

Case study: Yenn

I used to have a friend who I can now only describe as toxic. While she was autistic, she was also highly confrontational and rude. I always felt uncomfortable about being in her company but couldn't put my finger on what was wrong. She was possessive and petty. She would argue with me about certain topics so I would avoid those topics. She would then just argue with me about other topics. As someone who dislikes confrontation, I couldn't understand what was happening. She used to insist that I visit her every year when I had a regular presentation. I dreaded these visits as she would just boss me around and bully me. I still couldn't see that she was not a true friend. The last time I saw her she was so awful that I distanced myself from her. She was apparently very angry and possessive in response. She attacked me on my social media using a fake profile. I was really anxious about this but in the end she must have got over it as I haven't heard from her in years. Many of my other friends told me she was a toxic narcissist and I think they are right. Now I am more cautious about who I let into my life.

Advocacy with friends can mean increasing their knowledge about neurodiversity. You can use your experiences to support knowledge and understanding in your friends. You can help them understand other neurodivergent people better. Your advocacy with friends can make a big difference beyond your friendship.

Advocacy with family members

Family relationships can involve a range of experiences and interactions. Sometimes families are supportive and respectful – and often families have more than one neurodivergent member. It is often easier to set boundaries and call out poor behaviour in a supportive family. However, even in supportive families, issues can arise.

Some families involve very fraught and problematic interactions. The authors know an autistic man who has an extremely difficult relationship with his mother. The mother doesn't 'get' his autism and is judgemental of this man's autistic traits. The relationship is almost entirely negative and the efforts of this man to reach out to his mother and share his perspective simply haven't worked. Sometimes advocacy with family can be harder than advocacy with strangers.

Relationships with family can change over time. Yenn had a very challenging early life and relationships with their family were strained for many years. Yenn and their family worked on their relationships and now have a very positive relationship. This would not have happened without a lot of work from both sides. It took several years and a lot of give and take to get to this point. This is not to say that there are no issues, but the relationship is stronger so when issues arise they are addressed. This relationship building takes give and take from both parties.

Advocacy within families does not always relate only to neurodivergence; it can be more holistic than that and encompass other elements of life. Family members are likely to have known us pre-diagnosis and have a range of memories of us at young ages. Family relationships can be more intense than other relationships. This can be a positive or a negative thing – or a mix of both.

We often place more value on having a good relationship with family than with others, which can make a difficult family relationship all the more upsetting. Not being listened to or respected by family can seem much worse than not being respected or heard by friends or colleagues. Some families have a very strong deficits approach to neurodivergence. 'Warrior parents' and those seeking a cure for neurodivergent conditions can be really harmful to impressionable neurodivergent people. Some 'therapies' such as applied behaviour analysis (ABA) which some parents subject their children to can be traumatic and leave children damaged and possibly resenting their parents for using them. Many parents do not realize that these sorts of 'therapies' are harmful, but they can cause a rift in families and make relationships highly problematic.

As a society, we place a lot of emphasis on the value of family. However, for some people family is not a safe place. Many LGBTQIA+ people in particular have strained or damaging relationships with family members and some are ostracized and cut off. Some family relationships are not worth working on, particularly if they are toxic and damaging. If this is your family then advocacy may not actually be of much benefit as a degree of respect and listening is required in order for it to be effective. Consider finding a 'family of choice', grieve for your biological family if you need to, and move on to a world where you don't have to please people who won't listen to you or respect you. Reflect that society's emphasis on family relationships isn't always very helpful.

Advocacy and visitors

Having people over to your home can, at times, be a challenging and overwhelming experience. This is where it is vital to have a good sense of what you can tolerate, what your boundaries are and when you have had enough.

Ideally, when we have people visit, it needs to be on our terms. We need to be clear as to when they can come and visit and for how long.

Otherwise, what starts out as a pleasant experience can quickly turn into a rather stressful one.

Things to consider when inviting people to your home:

- Be clear on what time they can arrive and when they need to leave by.
- Don't feel pressured into having them stay longer.
- If you are feeling stressed or overwhelmed, politely ask your guests to leave, explaining that you have enjoyed spending time with them, but you are feeling tired and would like to spend some downtime alone to recharge. If possible, let them know that you will catch up with them again soon, and will let them know in the future when that will be.
- Consider how many people you want to see at one time. Do you find it easier on a one-on-one basis or in a small group of people?
- Consider if you want to be playing music or watching TV with them. Will the extra noise increase your levels of sensory stress?
- When having people in your home, make sure you set the boundaries and conditions. Your home, your rules! Stick by them.

Unexpected visitors

Now this is something many autistic people dread – the arrival of someone at the front door, unexpected and without being invited. Your first thoughts are who is this, did I forget someone was coming over? I hope they haven't seen me through the window. Where can I hide in my home so they don't see me, holding my breath so I don't make a noise? I hope they go away and think I am not at home!

Many of us can relate to these internal fearful thoughts that race through our minds as we hear the knocking on our door or the ringing of our doorbell. The reason we experience fear, rather than being excited someone has come to visit us, is that we don't like unexpected things happening, or surprises. These things are always out of our control and we like to have control of our environment and what is happening in our lives, so we can reduce our anxieties. When things are unknown or we don't know what the consequences are, we easily get highly anxious as we can't ascertain what the outcome of the experience will be. If things are not clear to us, it raises our anxiety and increases our overthinking, which is often based in negative thoughts rather than positive ones and if left unchecked evolves into catastrophizing. Once we hit the catastrophizing level, it becomes very difficult to rationalize the situation. And this can all happen in a matter of minutes.

What can you do when unexpected people turn up at your door? Well, you can resort to hiding until they are gone, but this doesn't stop the fear of 'what if they come back?' As difficult as it seems, it is always best to open the door to see who it is, unless it is in the middle of the night and then it is always best to shout out, 'Who is it?' before opening the door. Always think safety first! You can do this at any time prior to opening the door too. It will give you a few seconds to register in your mind who that person is and how you will react to them.

This is where setting good boundaries is a must, as is being firm in saying no to the person at the door if you do not want to invite them in. You do not need to give them a reason as to why you do not want them to come into your house at that time. If you do let them in, be clear in how long they can stay for. You may only want them there for 15 minutes. Tell them that. When it gets to the 15 minutes, tell them it is time to go and let them know that you need to plan for your next catch-up so you can spend more time together. But only if you want to do that!

Once you know what your limits are and you're firm in setting boundaries and saying no, the easier it will become to spend time with people in your home. Plan where possible and still do what works for you.

Case study: Barb

I have always disliked people turning up unexpectedly and would run and hide in my bedroom when they knocked on the door. My fear was often driven by the negative thoughts of having people coming into my home and judging me on how tidy I kept it. I had perfectionistic views on how my home should look and how everything needed to be clean and in its place. But I always felt as if my housekeeping skills were not good enough and that the place was far too untidy to have people to visit.

I am also highly sensitive to criticism due to past experiences and of the high standards I put on myself in everything I do. So, I never felt good enough for what I would perceive as other people's standards.

Also, I also feared that I would have no idea what to say to the person if I let them into my home. I needed time to prepare for any visits to my home so that I could put myself into the right headspace to talk to people, to reduce my anxiety beforehand as best I could, as I know these situations raise my anxiety, and to plan some topics that we could talk about, as I struggle to engage in general chit-chat about non-specific topics.

Over time, I learned to put in place boundaries around when people could visit and for how long, and I always tell people to not turn up unexpectedly to my home as I find it very difficult to cope. I need structure and planning in my life so I can be the best version of myself when they do visit.

I also emphasize that I am not being difficult, but that I am doing this so that everyone has a good time when we get together. Also, when I can plan, I make sure I have drinks and snacks that we all like, and I tidy my home so that I don't feel constantly anxious about a couple of dirty dishes in the sink and can focus on the person I am with. Knowing my limitations and expectations has made getting together with people a much more rewarding experience.

CHAPTER 8

Advocacy and a Public Profile

There are a large number of methods through which you can practise advocacy. These range from high-visibility, high-profile events to private discussions with friends or colleagues. A lot of people start small and work up from there, while others remain quite low profile and small scale. No one method of advocacy is 'better' than another and it really is about finding what method or methods work for you. This chapter covers information for people who want to practise their advocacy in the public domain.

When practising advocacy, it is best to play to your strengths. If you enjoy writing, then blogging or writing or contributing to books might be the best approach. If you have a job which is supportive of your advocacy, this may involve talking to your colleagues and managers about neurodiversity. If you are interested in the kind of advocacy that involves being a public figure, it often takes several years to build a profile within the community. However, this doesn't mean that other advocacy activities are not valuable or that you need to be a public figure to be an effective advocate. You can be an effective advocate by supporting another neurodivergent person, perhaps by attending a medical appointment with them or speaking on their behalf in education or work settings. Alternatively, of course, you can advocate for yourself in a variety of settings.

Advocates come in all shapes and sizes and with a huge range of activities and interests. Being well known is definitely not a prerequisite for advocacy, and indeed some high-profile advocates do damaging things and the community would be better off without their work. Conversely, some advocates with no public profile whatsoever help a lot of people. Integrity and humility are important qualities for neurodiversity advocates.

Social media presence

These days there are a lot of social media platforms, all of which have a different focus and audience. These can be a great forum for public advocacy, if that is something you are interested in doing. Many neurodivergent people are active on social media and a lot of advocacy happens there. Some platforms are used more by younger people while some appeal to older people. The different platforms allow for different sorts of posts and discussions. Facebook, for example, has a lot of functionality around groups and pages. There are a lot of neurodiversity groups on Facebook and on other social media platforms which have different options for engagement. Most people find one or two platforms which work well for them and enable them to share their advocacy messages and discussions. Many established advocates maintain a presence on a number of different social media platforms, which allows them to share their message in a slightly different way across these platforms and reach a wider and more diverse audience. Social media can enable you to reach a lot of people very quickly. It is a great way to build and promote your advocacy message and engage in discussions with other advocates and neurodivergent people.

A social media presence can take a while to establish. Do not be disheartened if your social media pages don't immediately or quickly generate thousands of followers. There are a lot of other advocates online and building an audience can take time. It helps to be appreciative of your existing followers and develop relationships with your more enthusiastic supporters. Yenn has people on their Facebook who have been there since they set up their page in 2007! This kind of loyalty is lovely, and these people can promote your work with their own followers. While social media is set up to make you excited about new followers and 'likes', it helps to remember that quality in interactions is usually preferable to quantity.

Social media can be challenging. There are a lot of trolls out there and they can make your online world very unpleasant. It can sometimes be hard to ascertain if an adverse comment is trolling or simply someone entering into a dialogue in an abrupt manner. If it feels wrong, then it probably is. And you owe nothing to anyone online, especially trolls. The block function is there for a reason! You do not have to engage in conversation with anyone and particularly people who are making hostile comments. They do not matter. Block them and move on.

Advocates can find themselves on the receiving end of a lot of other unhelpful online behaviour too. Scams can happen a lot, some of which are quite sophisticated. You can also get other people wanting to enlist your support for their online vendetta against someone – look out for people giving an ultimatum, wanting you to block or unfriend a person they are having a feud with. Sometimes people will post something they want to promote directly on your page without asking you. And sometimes people will engage in draining or triggering encounters. All of these situations require a degree of assertiveness to address! Despite these potential issues, the online world can be a great space for advocacy, and you can make a real difference with advocacy on social media.

Setting up an online group or social media page

If you would like to be an advocate in the public domain, one great way to engage in advocacy on social media is to create a page or group. This can be done relatively easily and doesn't require a lot of technical skill. Before setting up your page or group consider the following:

- Who is your intended audience? You can follow other groups and pages that you like which can attract others to your page.
- What content do you want to share on your page or group? Do you just want to post your own content, or do you want to share content from other groups or individuals?
- Make a list of individuals to invite to like/join your page. These can be friends but can also be other advocates or neurodiversity advocacy groups.
- What rules/parameters do you want for those interacting with your page/group? This is an important consideration and can help manage issues before they arise.

- What sorts of interactions do you want to have with your audience? Do you want to engage the audience actively (such as through giveaways or competitions) or passively?
- Do you want to ask a friend or colleague to help with the admin on your page or group? If you do, make sure you trust them as it is a big step to allow someone access to your page.
- Do you want to limit group members to only neurodivergent people?

Online pages and groups can be a great place to do advocacy. It can involve a lot of engaging discussions and you can get a message out to a lot of people. It is also good to be a part of the online neurodivergent community and contribute to the broader discussion. There are some issues which can arise with online pages and groups. These include trolling, vendettas/feuds among members, and people posting inappropriate or offensive things. These issues can be mostly managed with clear parameters and boundaries, a degree of assertiveness and judicious use of the block function.

Giving presentations

Many advocates give presentations. These can range from talks for small audiences to speaking at large conferences. Many people find public speaking very anxiety-provoking but there are some strategies to help address this. You don't need to give presentations if you don't want to or feel unable to but it can be a great way of sharing your message and making a difference. Most people improve with practice so don't worry if your first talk isn't a TED talk! You can work up to doing talks to bigger audiences.

It can be difficult to get invited to speak when you first start out. It can help to do talks initially for smaller community groups rather than holding out for 'better' opportunities. In fact, with public speaking, bigger does not necessarily mean better. If you reach one person, that is a good outcome.

It pays to be prepared. Write your talk out – you can use bullet points, PowerPoint slides – or, if you are really brave, you can do it from memory! Practise your talk a few times before you give it. Even expert speakers do this, and it helps both with your nerves and also with the quality of the final talk. You can practise with an audience of a friend, family member or partner. Try to make your presentation engaging. Telling anecdotes and stories is a good way to engage your audience. Using images and video in your talk can also help with engagement.

If you want to speak at conferences and larger events, it often helps to submit an abstract rather than waiting for the organizer to contact you and invite you to speak. An abstract is basically a proposal to speak at an event. You will need to include the outline of what you want to talk about as well as biographical information on yourself. If your abstract is accepted, you will be given time to speak at the event.

Payment for presenting can be a fraught topic. Neurodivergent people are traditionally not paid for many events as there can be an attitude that allowing us to speak is 'doing us a favour'. This is not okay. If others are being paid to present, then we should be too. It should be noted with conferences that anyone who gains their spot through submitting an abstract is not paid – allistic and neurodivergent alike. However, if you are invited to speak you should be paid. Some neurodivergent people struggle with the assertiveness required to ask for payment. One thing you can do is prepare a payment schedule listing your fees for presentations of different lengths and give this to the organizers when you are invited to speak. This means the organizer has an idea of what you charge and it provides a starting point for the discussion around fees. Put simply, if someone invites you to speak, they should be paying you unless it is a fundraiser or charity event. Neurodivergent speakers are experts and should be paid as experts. It is ironic that advocacy can be required around payment in order to do advocacy!

Some tips for public speaking:

- Prepare, prepare, prepare.
- If you need to, take a friend/support person with you to your event.
- Remember that you have been asked to speak because your expertise is valued and sought after.
- Use the first three slides/bullet points to ground yourself. I start with a title slide followed by a biography and photos of me doing interesting things. By the time I have got through the first three slides the nerves have gone.

- Remember that the audience want to see you and they want you to do well.
- Make sure the technology works well before your presentation. Save your presentation on a USB stick, bring your laptop if you need to and test the technology well before you go onstage. If you are speaking at a conference, take your presentation on a USB stick to the IT services team at the venue well in advance of your talk.
- Print your slides or bullet points and take them with you to your talk.

Responding to requests for advice

People who are known as advocates often receive requests for advice. These can come from a variety of places, including allistic parents, neurodivergent people, professionals and friends and family. It can be quite anxiety-provoking being asked to provide advice, but it can also be seen as quite flattering. Advocates often worry that they don't have the expertise or that what they say might not be helpful. To counter this, reflect that someone has sought you out for your expertise and they are happy to hear what you have to say. Don't try to be anything you are not and just respond as best you can. You can also refer the person seeking advice to another neurodivergent advocate or individual if you think they have something useful to say. You might think you don't have much useful information to share but in fact you do. As a neurodivergent person you are an expert in the neurodiverse experience. You also don't see yourself from outside. The knowledge you have in your brain might not seem very exciting to you as you already know it. However, to others the information in your brain is probably really helpful. Try to reflect that you are an expert and that the knowledge you have is really useful for others.

One issue that advocates come up against is impostor syndrome. Also called impostor phenomenon or fraud syndrome, impostor syndrome is a term to describe the psychological experience of feeling as if you don't deserve your success and that you are a 'fraud'. It is very common, and many advocates experience it. One way to counter this is to reflect that neurodivergent people are the experts on being neurodivergent so someone contacting you is going to get authentic, genuine advice. Speak with friends or family that you trust to challenge your feelings of being an impostor or fraud. It can be hard to be objective about yourself, so seeking out others' opinions can help.

Media appearances

Sometimes advocates are asked to give media appearances. This is often a positive, but media can be a bit unpredictable. If you are asked to give a media presentation, then research the programme or publication you are going to be featured in. What sort of attitudes do they espouse? Have they done anything else in the disability or neurodiversity space and, if so, was it respectful and positive or discriminatory and ableist? This can determine whether you agree to do the presentation or not.

Media requests usually come from a producer or journalist contacting you. Turnaround times for media appearances can be quite tight and you may be asked to give an interview the same day or day after you are initially contacted.

It can be anxiety-provoking doing media appearances, especially if you haven't done them before. Encourage yourself by thinking that they came to you for your opinion and that you have a lot of useful things to say. You can also reflect that you are helping a lot of people through the experience.

Writing with persuasion

Some people use writing as a means of advocacy. There are a lot of autistic bloggers and authors. There is quite a lot of competition in this area. In the early days of the neurodiversity movement there were a few neurodivergent – particularly autistic – writers who published autobiographical material. Authors Donna Williams (Polly Samuel), Temple Grandin and Wenn Lawson, as well as Liane Holliday Willey and Jean Kearns Miller, all wrote accounts of their experiences as autistic people.

Now there are a large number of accounts of living as a neurodivergent person. In recent years, many neurodivergent authors have started writing about matters related to neurodivergence, providing factual information and guidance rather than personal stories. There are a number of publishing companies which specialize in autism or neurodivergence. If you want to write a book, it is worth doing some research about which company might be interested to publish it as well as whether there are similar publications which might compete with yours. Writing a book takes planning, consideration and, usually, research. It can help to have a co-author, especially if it is your first time writing a book.

Writing a book is a big commitment and definitely not for everyone. A lot of neurodivergent people have a blog. Blogging is a great outlet and means of communicating and influencing people's thinking. It can help to come up with a list of topics to blog about. Knowing where to share your blog is a critical consideration. One of the best places to share it is on social media. It can help to share to a regular set of groups online. There are netiquette considerations around sharing blogs which you will need to understand and consider when sharing material online. If you want to share on an online group, make sure you have a look at the group rules as some groups consider blogs to be self-promotion and do not allow them. Have a look at what is published in groups and gauge if your blog fits with the ethos of the group. You can even put a disclaimer when you post your blog saying something like 'I hope it is okay to post this here' or 'Please remove this post if it is not appropriate.'

In terms of writing and advocacy, it is important to ensure that your writing is persuasive and meaningful. Drafting and editing are both important parts of the process. There is a saying 'write drunk, edit sober', which is of relevance here. Basically, it means the drafting process is all about creativity and getting down all the ideas that you can whereas the editing stage is about analysis and consideration. Leave enough time to edit your work. It can help to have a view of what you want the piece to look like and use your editing time to mould the piece to that vision. If you are concerned about whether your writing is good and helpful, share it with friends or family and seek their feedback before posting it online. You will improve with practice. Writing well is a great asset for an advocate but it is something which can be learned.

Case study: Yenn

I write a regular blog and post it on social media. I have been doing this since 2014. I have learned a lot through writing the blog. I find when people give constructive feedback, I can get quite defensive but then when I think about it, I see the feedback is actually helpful. I would rather someone point out an issue than not as it means I can address it and anyone else who sees the post will get the benefit of the feedback. I sometimes get trolls on my blog posts which is upsetting, but I have learned that the block function is appropriate in these cases. I have had hundreds of thousands of views of my blog posts over the years. Blogging is one of my favourite parts of my advocacy work. Through my blog, I have connected with other autistic bloggers and now I can appreciate and learn from their work too.

Being paid for advocacy work

Some advocates are paid for their work involving writing, presentations and consultancy. This is a good thing and should be encouraged, especially in a world that often devalues neurodivergent experience. Payments for advocacy work are a bit haphazard though, with some organizations paying a lot and others not wanting to pay anything. With presentations, the rule of thumb is that if you are invited to speak then the organization booking you should pay you a speaker fee, plus travel and accommodation costs if you travel to give the presentation. If you apply to give a presentation at an event then usually you will be expected to pay for your own travel and accommodation and will not receive a fee. Sometimes neurodivergent speakers are paid less than allistic presenters. This is not okay. With writing, it is a bit more complex. Some organizations which ask you to contribute an essay or blog post will pay you, but others won't. With books, if you author or co-author a book, you should be paid a royalty – usually a percentage of profits from the book. If you write a chapter or foreword, you will usually not be paid. With consultancy, it is also a bit complex, with some organizations paying and some not. You are within your rights to ask about payment and to request payment but not all organizations will pay you.

If someone asks you to speak at an event, deliver consultancy services or write a piece for them, always ask about whether there is a payment for the work. It helps to have a payment or fee schedule which you can show to the organization that wants to book you. Advise that you can be flexible with fees when you provide the fee schedule. Being paid is one way of demonstrating the value which organizations place on advocates. Organizations which pay allistic people for their work but not neurodivergent people are probably not very helpful or respectful. You could also talk with other advocates about how they approach payment and asking for fees. Discuss, if they are willing, how much they charge for talks and writing, whether they are flexible and negotiate with organizations booking them, and which organizations have been good to work with – and which haven't! Here is an example of a fee schedule. You can base your fee schedule on this if you would like to, or you can develop your own which better suits your circumstances.

Fee schedule – example
Presentation/facilitation/workshop fees
1 hour or less: $500
1–2 hours: $700
2–4 hours: $1000
Full day: $2000

Note: *These fees cover preparation and delivery of presentation/workshop. This relates to both onsite events and those conducted online.*

Consultancy/advice
$70 per hour

Writing – articles, blog posts and so on
$200 for between 800 and 1200 words.

Costs/reimbursements
[Speaker] will require the following costs either paid before the event or reimbursed:

- *Return economy flights to location.*
- *One night of accommodation for each day they are required at the event.*

Taxi/Uber

- *From their home to the airport, and return.*
- *From the airport at the location city to the accommodation (or venue if going there directly from the airport).*

Evidence for accommodation, flights and ground transport will be provided with the invoice.

Please contact me with any questions about fees, costs or invoices.

Email:
Phone:

CHAPTER 9

Knowing What Works for You in the Environment

Being able to determine what works best for you at home, at school and at work and being able to self-advocate around this is another incredibly important aspect you need to consider. Your environment can affect your ability to concentrate and perform your best at work. If your home environment is not designed for your needs, this can impact on your well-being and ability to relax and unwind. For example, at home you may be using bright ceiling lights as your partner or parents may prefer bright light to read, but this bright light doesn't work for you and your senses feel overwhelmed by it.

What you can do is self-advocate in this situation through compromise. Suggest that it would be better for everyone who uses that room to have lamp near where they are sitting so they can still see well to read, but the overall lighting in the room will be reduced. This is a win for everyone and considers everyone's needs. The same strategy can also be applied in the workplace or at school. Identify things like bright lights, where are they placed, and whether they can be turned off, replaced or a substitute used to best support all employees or students.

Some of the things to consider

At home

- Lighting of rooms. Does the lighting need to be changed to lamps? Can dimmer swtiches be installed?
- A quiet space. Do you have a quiet space that you can retreat to?

We all need a space that is welcoming and calming, especially when we become overwhelmed, stressed or anxious. Ideally this will be your 'safe space'.

- Clothing. Are your clothes making you uncomfortable or are you wearing certain clothes just to make other people happy? Consider what feels good for you and make changes to your wardrobe. You need to feel comfortable, not to make other people feel comfortable about how you look.
- Aversion to smells. These can be things like chemical cleaning products, personal hygiene products and bins. Do these need to be changed to non-scented or naturally scented products?
- Clutter. Is clutter impacting on your mental well-being? Where possible, declutter. The less you have to worry about, the easier it is for you to think. Ask family or friends to help you if you are struggling on deciding what you really need and don't need.
- Get help. Hire people where possible to do things that you struggle with, such as cleaning your kitchen, mowing, garden maintenance, car maintenance. Often these things are not too expensive and can take the huge pressure off your shoulders of having to keep on top of having a clean home or a car that runs as it should. When you fall behind it can be really hard to get back on top of things. If you cannot afford to hire someone, maybe ask a friend to swap chores. You may enjoy vacuuming and tidying up rooms and your friend may enjoy cleaning bathrooms and kitchens. Make it fun and creative. Asking someone to come and clean your house with you can make it a much less overwhelming task.

At school

- Noisy classroom. Is there a way the noise can be reduced? If not, can you use things like ear pods/headphones to reduce the noise for you? To advocate for the need to wear the ear pods/headphones throughout class it is best to speak directly with the teacher/lecturer and explain your needs. Good teachers/lecturers will completely understand.
- Lighting. Can the lighting be changed? If not, can you move to another place that is not so bright? If you are restricted in where

you can sit, wear tinted glasses to reduce the glare. Again, speak directly to the educator as to why you need to do this.

- Distractions. Is sitting near windows going to affect your learning and concentration? Where possible, move to a place in the room that will reduce your distractions. Also consider this if you have exams in rooms with windows. Give yourself the best chance at succeeding through the reduction of distractions.
- Break times. Do you prefer to have a quiet space to have lunch? You may need to ask the teacher if there is a room where you can eat quietly. Also, be clear to people that you would prefer to spend your break times quietly to help you prepare mentally for the next class. If you let them know that this is why you are taking time out for yourself, it can also reduce the assumption that you appear to be ignoring them or not wanting to be with them. Again, you can also compromise by saying that you will meet with them for the lunch break only, not the morning and afternoon breaks. Do what works best for you!

At work

- Travelling to and from work. Does this add to your daily overwhelm? Travelling on noisy public transport can be overwhelming, so be prepared with things like ear pods and headphones to reduce noise. If you drive, traffic can be overwhelming, so consider getting to work earlier where possible. Ask your boss if you can start an hour earlier and leave an hour earlier to avoid peak traffic times. Ask a co-worker if they would be happy to drive you to and from work to reduce the need to concentrate on traffic. But do make sure they are a good driver, otherwise it could add to your stress!
- Lighting. Again, consider the lighting and where best to sit in the office if possible. Speak to co-workers to see if they would prefer to move to a spot you least like. They may prefer bright areas and you can swap them for their darker part of the office.
- The lunchroom. Is this noisy and uninviting? Are there too many people talking, is the hum of the fridge too loud, is the air-conditioning too cold? These are factors to consider when taking a break. You want to feel refreshed, not further stressed.

Let co-workers know you will meet them for lunch elsewhere, for example a quiet park, and that you find the lunchroom too noisy, but also you think it would be good for everyone to get outside for some fresh air!

• Your workstation. Design your work area to best suit you. Consult with your boss if you need to make adjustments to the design or layout. Usually, when you explain that you are changing things to help you better perform at your job, they will be more than happy for you to make the changes.

Case study: Katie – Environmental/ sensory workplace audit

Katie is a 39-year-old woman, recently diagnosed with autism level 1 and dyslexia. Katie sought a diagnosis after a lifetime of challenges with school and employment, including difficulty keeping a job, making friends and being subjected to bullying both at school and in the workplace. She expressed having difficulty staying focused when she was at work, and this led to her losing her job on numerous occasions, due to reoccurring minor mistakes. Katie didn't understand why she kept making mistakes and why she couldn't remember all the details or complete correctly the tasks given to her.

Katie often suffered from headaches and felt overwhelmed and exhausted at the end of the working day. She experienced meltdowns at home, especially if her train was late or extremely crowded heading home, which tipped her 'over the edge'. She was often anxious and depressed due to her constant mistakes and failings at work. When Katie asked for help at work in the past she was treated poorly, with the employer stating that she should know how to do simple tasks without regular monitoring and repeated questions.

She was extremely anxious she would lose her most recent position in administration but was afraid to ask for support and feedback on her progress due to this previous incident. However, Katie felt that she had a better understanding of herself since gaining a diagnosis. She wished to understand more about her sensory profile and how to implement strategies to help her at work and to become more confident in advocating for her support needs without feeling there would be repercussions or humiliation.

Katie's workplace was on the 11th floor of a multistorey building, set within a medium office space in a designated workstation cubicle. There were six cubicles and employees within this room. The office space was brightly lit with large, double-tubed fluorescent lighting and three medium-size windows on the far-left side of the room. Katie's cubicle was positioned furthest away from the windows in a line of three. Her cubicle walls were light grey in colour and her desk had a white gloss surface. Her computer screen was 21 inches in size and the programs she used were Microsoft Word, Excel and an in-house specialized software for data collection and quotations.

Five-minute screen breaks were given each hour, with a 15-minute morning tea break and 45-minute lunch break. During these breaks, Katie stayed at her desk checking her phone and social media. The only times she moved from her desk were to go to the toilet or to collect her lunch from the fridge in the adjoining lunchroom.

Katie's work hours were from 9am to 4.15pm, Monday to Thursday. Her train journey to work was 50 minutes, with a 10-minute walk to her workplace from the station. It was a 15-minute walk to the station from her home.

Katie's sensory profile indicated she that she was sensory avoidant and visually overwhelmed by bright lighting, computer screens and light-coloured reflective surfaces. This led to her difficulty in retaining information from assigned tasks as the day progressed. It was also contributing to her regular headaches and feelings of overwhelm and exhaustion at the end of the working day. These factors combined to make Katie hypervigilant and extremely anxious, and her low threshold for tolerating bright lighting compounded her problems throughout the day, leading to her overwhelm at the end of the day, resulting in meltdowns.

Workplace design recommendations

The workplace had neutral colours of light grey walls, work desks were white with a glossy surface, and the carpet was a medium grey, unpatterned. There were few items on the walls. Six workstation cubicles were in two lines of three, with Katie's workstation in the second row on the right-hand side. The rows faced the northern wall and the three medium-sized windows had roller blinds that were adjusted when there was afternoon sun. Afternoon sunlight shone through these windows from approximately 1pm until employees ceased work.

The lighting consisted of three rows of double fluorescent tubes. Each row of lights could be individually turned on and off. Two of these rows sat above the two rows of workstations.

Each workstation cubicle consisted of one desk with a drawer, an adjustable office chair, a non-slip mat under the chair, a desktop computer with a 21-inch flat-screen monitor, a headset and a two-drawer filing cabinet. Employees were allowed to personalize the decor of their workstations.

Solutions

Katie suffered from regular headaches and extreme anxiety. Research has shown a strong link between migraines and anxiety and suggests there is a correlation from these physical experiences caused by sensory hyperactivity (Lane *et al.*, 2009). Sullivan and colleagues (2014) highlighted that some individuals are over-reactive to sensory input, contributing to anxiety and migraines.

It was recommended that Katie's workplace turned off sections of lighting and that the employer discussed with the other five employees within the room what their preference was in the level of lighting needed. If one row of three individuals preferred less lighting, the fluorescent lights above this row could be turned off.

Katie's workstation was moved to the end of the row, nearest the windows to allow for more natural lighting and to benefit from the afternoon sunlight after a morning of artificial lights. This reduced some of her mental fatigue and the onset of headaches. Each individual workstation also had access to a lamp with lower wattage and warm colour to provide more lighting, for example when reading paper documents.

As each workstation could have individual changes to decor, it was suggested that Katie used a dark-coloured cloth or covering for her desk to reduce the glare from the white glossy surface of the desk.

Katie's computer monitors were adjusted to a lower brightness. The software programs she used had a significant amount of white space working area, which was adjusted by changing the design background and theme colours to a more suitable colour.

Workplace awareness

Katie's workplace had limited knowledge of autism but was willing to work together with Katie in making her workstation design more accommodating to her needs. Her employer was open to understanding how to become a more inclusive workplace, but the company was on a strict budget for modifications and training.

The accommodations and rearranging of where Katie's workstation was placed in respect to ceiling and natural lighting did not incur equipment costs. Redesigning the layout benefited Katie and her colleagues by providing the light conditions that they preferred. A lamp for each workstation was inexpensive to implement.

Helping Katie to understand how to adjust the light intensity of her monitor screen and to tailor software program background colours and themes also helped to reduce light sensory input. This, combined with a new workstation position and dark covering to Katie's desk, reduced her visual issues significantly.

It was recommended that the employer undertook a structured meeting with Katie, and provided her with an agenda two weeks beforehand, to allow Katie enough time to prepare notes and questions.

Autistic people often experience challenges in conveying their needs and supports due to misunderstandings through communication differences. This also gives rise to increased anxiety levels, which Katie already experienced due to past negative experiences. A mediator, chosen by Katie to attend the meeting with her, helped her to convey her needs and supports effectively. It also helped Katie understand what her employer expected from her in return.

As Katie suffered from severe anxiety due to past employer experience, this mediator helped Katie to feel more at ease in explaining her needs and to understand how the employer could work with her. Regular feedback from the employer on Katie's performance gave her a better insight into how she was doing with her work and identify patterns that were leading to mistakes. Identifying the patterns assisted in finding resolutions to these mistakes.

Recognizing Katie's support needs

With regard to downtime for Katie, her workplace was on the 11th floor of a multicomplex and she felt she was limited during the day in finding another space where she could relax. She felt safest within her own workstation as it was familiar and she was not bothered by the other employees. Katie did not feel comfortable having her lunch in the designated lunchroom as other employees were there and the lighting was extremely bright. Katie felt inadequate in joining in conversations with fellow employees as she often didn't know what to say and was extremely self-conscious.

During her initial meeting with the employer and mediator, suggestions for how to provide Katie with a place to have breaks away from her workstation were considered. Katie needed to have a safe place where she could relax and have a mental break from screen time. As Katie did not feel safe going to the lunchroom, she was increasing her screen time by staying at her workstation and spending time on her phone as a means of distraction. This extra screen time added to Katie's visual sensory issues.

To help Katie reduce this time, negotiation with her employer about when she could take her screen breaks and lunch break was instrumental in her gaining alone time within the lunchroom. Having Katie's breaks allocated to different times from the rest of the employees meant that she felt safe within the lunchroom and could quietly eat her lunch. Having a lamp within the lunchroom allowed for Katie to turn off the bright fluorescent lighting.

Katie said that if she couldn't have this quiet time alone, she was prepared to also listen to a mindfulness app on her phone or to calming music, instead of spending time on social media.

Working together was the key to Katie's success in the workplace and helped her gain back her self-esteem, self-determination and the confidence to self-advocate for her needs and supports. The reduction of her visual sensitivities also helped with the reduction of her headaches, anxiety and the chance of having a meltdown at the end of the working day.

The employer was prepared to undertake online training. The employer discussed with internal Human Resources the opportunity of having key employees undertake the training to help them understand autism and how to give 'on the floor' support to autistic employees.

Outcomes

The sensory/environmental audit and discussion with Katie's employer, and their willingness to support Katie at work, meant that there was a positive outlook for Katie and future autistic employees. Katie was prepared to implement strategies to support herself in the workplace by having tinted glasses to wear if the lighting was too bright or if she was in situations where the lighting could not be reduced.

Katie requested that the employer provided her with coloured pens, sticky tabs and notepads so she could make notes as she came across difficulties; for example, she would use the sticky tabs as reminders to find places within documents, and coloured pens to remind her of a specific task allocated to a specific colour.

To cover the workstation desk with a dark material, Katie visited the local market to purchase textured material that was also pleasant for her to touch. Katie had not indicated textural sensitives but having a material that was pleasant to touch added to her positive and calming environment.

Katie obtained a diary to keep a daily record of times of day when she was feeling overwhelmed, tired or could sense the onset of a headache, along with noting the type of task and lighting she had at that point in time. This helped Katie recognize if there was a pattern to when these things happened and she could consider what strategies she would need to implement in helping to reduce them.

A follow-up sensory/environmental audit occurred after three months. Outcomes were positive, and Katie's workplace was becoming one that was supportive and educated on how to provide an inclusive and sensory-friendly working environment.

CHAPTER 10

Advocacy Study: Autism Leadership and the Online World

The explosion of social media in the past 13–15 years has seen the rise of online communities where marginalized and/or isolated individuals connect with like-minded people who provide support, friendship and solidarity. Often, these people would not experience these connections in everyday life and one such group is people on the autism spectrum. Autistic people have discovered that online platforms can give them an arena to voice their opinions among people they consider to be part of their 'tribe'. This connection gives them a sense of purpose, belonging and a place where their voice will be heard, taken seriously and understood by those who have similar experiences, seen as comrades.

With this evolution of online communities, leaders in the form of autism advocates have emerged. Their voices unite fellow autistic people, and their passion to support fellow tribe members gives them a sense of responsibility and accountability. These advocacy leaders endeavour to find ways to show the wider community, through social media, the value and worth of the autistic community. They demand change within society to break down barriers and to open up opportunities for all, to alter societal perspectives of autism, and to accept neurological divergence as something different, not broken or defective.

But along with this leadership in advocacy come challenges from certain people and organizations that propose to support people on the autism spectrum but are in fact doing harm in a variety of ways. Their limited knowledge and often dismissive and dehumanizing views on the abilities of autistic people are an obstacle for autism advocates.

These unhelpful stakeholders can come in the form of non-autistic parents (often referred to as 'warrior parents'), or on occasion parents of autistic children with high support needs who feel their voice is lost among the more vocal autism advocates, claiming they do not understand, nor are like, their child. These parents can be overwhelmed with emotion, stressed and have experienced a severe a lack of support. They miss golden opportunities to embrace the autistic voices that genuinely want better outcomes for their child and instead view autism advocates as the enemy.

Another challenge for advocates is those health professionals – counsellors, psychologists, psychiatrists – who perceive autism through a medicalized and deficits-based model, and fail to focus on autistic strengths. Other therapists, for example proponents of the 'evidence-based' model of applied behavioural analysis (ABA), promote their intensive programmes as giving positive outcomes for young autistic children, but many autistic adults view this support as abusive and detrimental to the long-term mental health of those who go through it. There is evidence to demonstrate that those going through ABA as children have suffered from post-traumatic stress disorder and extended periods of depression, and that this is related to their experience of ABA.

Some disability organizations have few or no autistic voices to inform their decision-making, so autistic perspectives are excluded. In research and academia, funding and research are often focused on what causes autism and how autism can be 'fixed', with minimal input from autistic voices in hearing what they want researched to help them in a world that is not genuinely inclusive of their differences. The autistic community can suffer due to a lack of research into health needs, how to reduce rates of suicide, how to turn around the significant unemployment rates – things which are paramount in creating a self-determined independent and fulfilling life for autistic people.

This leaves the question, how does the humble autism advocate, the leader among their autistic tribe who often takes responsibility on themselves for their community, address such significant factors with stakeholders and try to change their perceptions? How do advocates get these unhelpful influencers to step out of their comfort zone and try something new, or stop them from saying, 'Well, it is just too hard to implement'? This chapter will investigate how these autism advocacy leaders can effect productive change within the autistic and wider community.

Leadership

In today's information-hungry society, with the availability of online content, social media has become a successful means for individuals to collaborate on, discuss and instigate change within their community. Emerging autism leaders within online communities have progressively loosened the grip of the medicalized approach of certain health professionals that has overshadowed the community for many decades. Historically, doctors and scientists have inadvertently replaced the religious leaders of old, as the modern-day healers and saviours, and have shaped the experience of disability to conform to a medical model. The medical model reduces the capacity and function of those deemed 'disabled' and dehumanizes their existence.

In 1993, autism advocate Jim Sinclair delivered a distinctive message to parents of autistic children exclaiming, 'Don't mourn for us.' This was a pivotal point in history for autistic people stepping up and speaking out to claim their identities. Sinclair's message implicitly states that parents need to stop grieving for the loss of a perceived 'normal' child and looking for a cure, and, instead, embrace their unique child, with their strengths and challenges. He said that the autistic experience of the world is intrinsic to their identity and cannot be separated from them.

Since this evolutionary moment in history, where the depiction of autism was flipped from a medicalized model to one of social disability, autistic individuals have had the opportunity to feel a sense of pride in and, even more, a sense of control over, their own lives. No longer do they feel defined by their deficits, constrained to fit into a society that was never designed for them, and no longer do they need to mask their true selves. Autistic leaders have emerged around the world with an almost unanimous voice – that autistics are here, they deserve better treatment and acceptance within society, and, possibly most importantly, they are in charge of their identities, of defining who they are. This view, which dispenses with the perception that autistic people are destined for challenging, unfulfilled and difficult lives, focuses on what can be achieved and celebrated, and has been overwhelmingly embraced by the autistic community.

The concept of neurodiversity has brought to the fore the perception that neurological differences in thinking are an important factor for growth and diversity within society. Modern-day neurodiversity proponents advocate that all people on the autism spectrum, no matter the level of perceived impairment, have value and something to contribute to society. It is often viewed that society is failing individuals with high needs, but if they were given the right accommodations and different platforms to communicate through, they would have their own unique voice to determine their needs and visions for their own futures. Non-speaking advocates Carly Fleischmann and Amy Sequenzia, who without assistive technology would have no platform for the world to hear their voices, highlight that, with the right tools, all can have an effective voice to express themselves and to assert their needs.

Each autism leader, past and emerging, paves a way for the wider autistic community to stand up and have a voice. Their voices break down barriers to being accepted into society, whether it be through access to technology for communication, changing the way the workplace is designed, or expressing lived experiences through books, journals, blogs and social media. They enable society to have a better understanding of how these individuals perceive the world. These leaders have found their platform through social media. This platform has the ability to disseminate information quickly and garner support rapidly, especially when autism leaders step up and speak out. These individuals are the champions the autistic community aspire to, and are a strong collective voice.

A group of people who share a common concern or passion about a particular topic create the framework for a community of practice (CoP) (Wenger, McDermott & Snyder, 2002). With the increasing use of the internet and rapid expansion of networking through social media platforms, virtual communities of practice (VCoPs) have gained significant value in bringing together a wide range of stakeholders working towards a common cause or topic. VCoPs have become instrumental in allowing a wider collaboration of stakeholders that is not limited by locality and in-person only discussions. These online communities increase the inclusivity of individuals who were previously restricted by where they live or lack transportation to meetings, and assistive technologies enable the concerns of those with no or limited speech to be heard. These online communities also allow time for reflection and discussion at an individual's own processing pace.

Autism leaders can find support by creating a VCoP for their visions and expand their and the community's knowledge bank through sharing ideas, experiences and research. When an autism leader instils a sense of value to all contributing members of the VCoP, these very members become part of the support network for all. Sharing the common goal also provides opportunity for autistic people to self-advocate for their concerns and feel that their experiences are validated. The collective knowledge further supports all members of the VCoP.

These VCoPs can take many forms with a variety of stakeholders. For example, a VCoP that is exclusively autistic provides a platform for a variety of stakeholders within this domain. Stakeholders can be all autistic voices but also part of a women, men and gender-diverse community, the LGBTQIA+ community, individuals without speech, and individuals with varying support needs. Another VCoP could take on the wider audience of voices from parents, health professionals, educators, employment services and disability organizations, with the prominent focus on the autistic voice as this is often less heard, needs support in being heard and requires facilitation in self-advocacy. In each of these very different VCoPs, the autistic voice has to be the leader in directing what the stakeholders want for their lives.

Barriers to inclusion

Autistic individuals are confronted with an array of barriers in many situations throughout their life. These situations are centred around what wider society expects of all individuals, a one-size-fits-all model, without the distinct consideration of disability, difference and inclusion. With the added individual challenges of a lack of effective communication skills, a lack of self-advocacy and self-determination skills, and the overall impact of anxiety, feeling inadequate and lacking self-confidence, autistic people are desperate for their voices to be heard. These voices must therefore be acknowledged, respected and acted on in educational and employment settings, as these aspects of life heavily influence future outcomes. If autistic people are not set up for success, given the tools and strategies that they can implement to support and advocate for themselves, society is failing at providing pathways to include and value them.

The autistic community has clearly identified its barriers and is demanding a change in focus from all stakeholders that propose to support these individuals. Autism leaders need to encourage change in perspectives from all stakeholders, to learn from each other and to implement action plans that will change the current mindset to one that encompasses the views and needs of autistic people. Leaders need to challenge old perspectives with new ideas, face problems that they currently cannot find solutions to, and bring together all stakeholders to develop and learn new ways of implementing change.

Important changes occur when stakeholders have a goal and feel connected to a purpose. These changes need to start with educators listening to the parents and the autistic child's needs and supports, working with them collaboratively to find solutions that provide the best possible future. Young autistic adults need to be heard and supported in finding their voice so they can advocate for themselves, setting them up for adulthood and a future that they can determine for themselves. Employers need to work with autistic people in creating working environments that support them, consider their sensory needs, value their unique way of viewing the world and facilitate them in expressing new ideas and concepts that can effectively benefit all in the workplace.

Researchers and academics are slowly changing their perspectives of autism from the deficits-based model, investigating what they perceive as important in autism research by listening to autistic voices and including them in discussions and research projects. Precedence is now being given to how research can improve the lives of autistics, rather than searching for a 'fix' or cure.

Challenges for autism leaders

Autism leaders are the voice of the wider community, but they bear a huge weight of responsibility in the community, often without experience in leadership, and are unprepared in setting boundaries and implementing self-care. They may be highly susceptible to burnout.

Unfortunately, these autism leaders frequently feel the emotional pain of their supporters and are driven to do what they can, often at all hours, without the experience or implementation of good self-care, and to the detriment of their own personal well-being. Social media is always 'on'; somewhere around the globe, a follower, a desperate voice, will be in need of support. Instant notifications fill these individuals' inboxes and phone messages, adding to their desperation to help, without the insight or knowledge of how they can muster the wider community to work with them to support each other. The ability to work together as a community with an effective leader is something the autism advocacy realm is in dire need of developing.

A level of assertiveness skills and the ability to say no are essential tools in the advocate's kit, but not all advocacy leaders possess these skills. The nature of being autistic in modern society can make it harder to gain assertiveness skills, meaning that advocates can struggle in setting boundaries. There is also a perception by many that advocacy leaders have everything sorted out in their life and the nature of their leadership apparently means they not only need little or no support but also that it is okay to attack and challenge them. In fact, many autism leaders struggle with being triggered and trolled and require a lot of support and kindness to manage the work that they do.

Actions for change

Driving social change around autism and inclusion are the autism advocates, the leaders within the autistic community. They have lived these experiences and are passionate about change, not just for themselves, but for all within their community. This community often resembles family and many within it would do everything possible to see that fellow autistics do not suffer unnecessarily as they have in the past. These leaders demand change and the support for their community, and advocacy is often extensive and global.

Twitter hashtags, for example #ActuallyAutistic and #AskingAutistics, have been instrumental in educating, sharing experiences and validation with autistic people on a global scale. These hashtags bring together large numbers of the autistic community who may not necessarily know where to look for information when newly diagnosed, or where to find other like-minded people, or where to ask questions. Using these hashtags, a whole new world of information opens up to autistic people. These connections grow the community, provide opportunities for discussion and debate, and instil self-advocacy within each autistic person who comments or initiates discussion.

The autism advocacy leaders can be seen collectively unified under such hashtags, but each also with their own areas of expertise, experience or interest. Autistic academics and researchers are finding a platform within social media to evaluate current research, to discuss gaps within the research and to initiate research that they want undertaken for their community. This same social media platform also offers the opportunity to reach out to academics and researchers who would not have been accessible in the past. Discussion posts can tag people they want involved or to contribute, in an instant, instead of waiting days or weeks for email responses, highlighting the importance of near instant discussions of pressing topics.

These opportunities allow the community, and more so the autism leaders, to learn and grow their knowledge quickly and to implement this knowledge to facilitate change for the community. A good framework for leadership is one that is driven by enthusiasm, energy and hope, and has a sound basis with a moral purpose, builds relationships, and understands the necessity of change. Dedicated leaders will disseminate the knowledge before them and act in the best interests of their whole community. A good leader will provide a solid voice for all, acknowledging and representing the majority of the community they are dedicated to serve. A good leader will embark on alleviating isolation for marginalized individuals and provide solid evidence to stakeholders of how working together will be inclusive to all members of society. Advocacy leaders have compassion for their fellow autistic tribe members and will allow their voices to be heard. A leader that pushes for change, whether it is simple or complex, will ultimately engage the concerns and visions of all and will set the framework for all stakeholders to work together in effecting productive change.

The road to autism advocacy and leadership is one that is imbued with emotion, life experiences and compassion. Often, autism leaders within their community are not selectively chosen but evolve as they find their voice through discussion with fellow autistic individuals. They are driven by their passion to make meaningful change for all based on their lived experiences and those of their community. These leaders often come from a background of challenges, struggles and barriers that they have navigated through, while also letting down their masks (the facade autistics are so frequently expected to use to appease society), to be true to themselves and to the community, revealing the rawness of their existence. This genuine and starkly honest approach garners support from their autistic community, and barriers of communication difficulties that are experienced in society diminish when divulging to fellow autistics who are just like them. Autistic people – through the empowerment provided by their leaders – finally feel heard and are no longer afraid.

Autism leaders with good moral standing – those who validate the voices of their community and whose primary purpose is to serve their community in effecting positive and productive change – have a voice that must be heard, must be listened to, and, most importantly, must be acted on and embraced by all of society. These autism leaders are the catalyst for instigating change for the autistic community. It is time for society to sit up and listen.

CHAPTER 11

Considerations Around Advocacy

Arguments about advocacy

Advocates are sometimes on the receiving end of criticism or personal attacks. This is particularly true for advocates who are vocal and have a presence on social media. Trolling and abuse can be commonplace. It is not ever okay to troll a person, and particularly a neurodivergent person, but it happens. Being attacked can result in people giving up their public advocacy role, which is disappointing and not right. Sometimes arguments and criticism can come from advocate colleagues. There have been a number of notable public arguments between disability advocates, and these are really upsetting. Given that we face common adversaries – such as ableism and discrimination – it seems very wrong that we should attack one another, but it does happen.

You can't control what other people do but you can control your own behaviour and responses. It is best to be supportive of advocate colleagues and if they do something you feel is wrong then rather than publicly attacking them, private message them to discuss the issue. If someone attacks you then be mindful that what you share publicly will reflect on you so try to take the 'high ground' and respond in a way that is clear and definite but also respectful. We are not always going to agree and that is okay. But when disagreeing it is best to be respectful rather than harshly critical or insulting.

Sometimes in the public advocate world you will meet someone who pushes all your buttons and makes you feel angry and resentful. This is just basic human nature, and it is okay. But it is important to remember that people may well view you as a role model. Instead of being publicly critical of the person, just avoid being in places where they are. If you have to share space with them then try to avoid any negative comments or engagements. Being critical of fellow neurodivergent people is not a good example to set. It can help to vent privately to a friend if someone really bothers you. Remember that if you have a profile, it means that people are looking to you for leadership.

Advocacy of allistics on behalf of neurodivergent people

Sometimes allistic/neurotypical people advocate on behalf of neurodivergent people. This is a sensitive and complex area where sometimes it is appropriate and other times it is not. With children, and especially small children, it is usually appropriate for neurotypicals who have a degree of influence and responsibility for them (such as a parent) to perform some advocate roles. This includes situations with schools and with other parents. Young children often lack the skills, experience and confidence to be advocates for themselves. However, this does not mean that parents should not teach advocacy skills to their children. Children can learn to speak up for themselves and this is often a great and empowering thing. Parents can explain to children some of the issues around advocacy and help instil a sense of self-knowledge and pride in their kids. Parents can recognize that their child may not be an effective advocate for themselves but that this can and probably will change with support and increased experience of seeing their parents advocating for them. Self-advocacy is often more effective than someone advocating on your behalf. Parents can encourage a growing sense of pride and an ability for advocacy in their neurodivergent kids.

There are some situations where advocacy on behalf of neurodivergent people might not be appropriate:

- Standing up for someone who is capable of standing up for themselves.
- Going against the wishes or interests of the neurodivergent person.
- Not listening to the needs of the neurodivergent person as expressed by them.

- Speaking from a position of self-interest.
- Making assumptions about the neurodivergent person's wishes and needs.

Advocacy for someone other than yourself is not about 'doing for' but about 'doing with'. It needs to come from a position of inclusion and deep respect otherwise it is likely to be counterproductive and may even be harmful. Having an understanding of neurodiversity and intersectionality is essential for anyone doing advocacy on behalf of another person. Listening to their needs, wants and interests is also essential. Advocacy is about promoting the interests of marginalized people and as such needs to be entirely inclusive. It should support and empower people to be their authentic selves and should help people to overcome disadvantage and discrimination.

Ideally, people should self-advocate but in some instances, this is not possible. Where self-advocacy is not possible then it is essential that the person doing the advocacy is coming from a place of respect and inclusion and has the interests of the person they are advocating for front and centre. It is possible to support people to build their advocacy skills, as outlined in this book. The idea of 'nothing about us without us' is critical in this space. Neurodivergent people should be in control of their destiny as much as possible and should preferably be the ones speaking on their own behalf. However, this is not to say that allistic people should never advocate for them. As discussed, there are some instances where neurodivergent people may not be able to advocate on their own behalf. Allistic allies can be very helpful and co-advocacy – where an allistic person supports a neurodivergent person in their advocacy – can be effective in a number of situations:

- At work, particularly where there are conflicts or where performance issues are raised.
- Where someone is in mental health crisis or is very unwell.
- At school, where a neurodivergent student is having difficulties and cannot express their needs.
- In friendships, where the allistic person can act as a mediator and interpreter if needed.
- In legal situations such as at court, where the allistic person can act as an intermediary.

Warning signs/red flags for ableism

Some people claim to be allies and support neurodivergent people but in fact they have ableist attitudes and biases. They may be condescending, and their 'help' more platitudes and paternalism. They may also be controlling and overbearing and want to take over the advocacy work from the neurodivergent people. Or they may be hostile and consciously ableist. None of these attitudes is helpful and can actually put back the cause of genuine advocacy.

Case study: Yenn

I was asked to speak at a parents' forum in a regional area. The organization booking me offered payment and seemed at first to be very inclusive and autism positive. However, when I arrived at the town and the CEO of the organization met me I saw a different side. The CEO's attitude was quite condescending. I felt like a child. As we chatted, she asked me what I planned to wear for my talk. I was a bit taken aback by this question. Why would she ask such a thing? She then went on to tell me that the autistic speaker the year before had worn an 'inappropriate' skirt! I was horrified. She also complained about the 'hard-line activists' in the town. I was good friends with most of these 'hard-line activists'! It didn't end there either. After I gave my talk, we had a Q&A session. The CEO kicked off the questions with an absolute humdinger. She asked, 'What should we do about all the politically correct people who have hijacked the autism community?' I am proud of my response! I said that attacks on so-called 'political correctness' were attacks on inclusion and respect and who wants to be disrespectful? My 'hard-line activist' friends were delighted.

This story highlights the issue of well-meaning people having a load of unconscious – and sometimes conscious – biases around neurodiversity. I did not feel as if I was an important part of the event. I felt like a token autistic. I felt as if the organization knew they should include autistic voices but they were not really all that respectful of actual autistic people. I wondered what kinds of lives their kids must have had.

Different sorts of ableist people require different approaches:

- Consciously hostile and toxic people. The best strategy with this group is to avoid them where possible. Nothing you say is likely to change their views. If you have to engage with these people, then put in place some supports for yourself. Have a friend, family member or colleague who you can vent to and seek support from. Remind yourself that the hostile person is the problem and not you. You may need to call them out on their behaviour but make sure you have support when you do.
- Condescending people. Often these attitudes are unintentional and unknown. This means that if you call the person out on it they may be quite surprised and, more importantly, they are likely to become defensive in response. Try to bring these people along with you on the journey. They are usually not particularly hostile but be careful how you approach any conversations around their attitudes. It can help to talk to a trusted person – friend, family member, partner – about the best way to have the conversation. Often these conversations come from an initial comment about how the paternalism makes you feel. That is often more helpful than a conversation around 'You need to stop behaving this way...'
- People with unconscious ableism. Unconscious bias is particularly tricky to address because it is, well, unconscious! People guilty of this often have no idea that they are being ableist, which makes it very difficult to address their unconscious bias. There are courses people can do to address and recognize their unconscious biases, but the person needs to realize that they need this training before they will undertake it! Unconscious bias often comes from a position of privilege. If someone doesn't face prejudice and stigma themselves, they are less likely to recognize what discrimination looks like. Unconscious bias can result in the use of ableist language and slurs, exclusionary behaviour or actual discrimination. It is helpful to call out someone for unconscious bias but it needs to be done carefully as they most likely don't realize that there is an issue.

Case study: Mel

Mel is a 32-year-old autistic woman. She has two nieces aged one and three. Mel's dad has a lot of unconscious bias around autism and disability more generally. When Mel was visiting family, her dad said of her three-year-old niece, 'Isn't it good that she is so normal?' Mel was very upset by this and said 'Normal compared to what, Dad? Normal compared to me?' Her dad got quite defensive, and it led to difficulty in the relationship between Mel and her dad. Mel didn't know how to get through to her dad because he couldn't see why Mel viewed his comment as a very problematic statement.

Advocacy conversations with individuals

A lot of self-advocacy revolves around conversations with individuals. Often these individuals are at a different point in their journey of knowledge about neurodiversity than the advocate they are speaking with. This can be quite challenging for neurodivergent advocates. Sometimes people will have no idea that they are being disrespectful for saying ableist things. The concept of microaggressions is often relevant here. Microaggressions are indirect and often unintentional insults. Examples include, 'You don't look dyslexic' or 'You could pass for normal.' They can be very upsetting and difficult. They come from a place where a person lacks understanding and knowledge and they are very common.

Being able to respond effectively to microaggressions is a very useful part of advocacy. Assertiveness and boundary-setting are key weapons in your arsenal of defences against microaggressions. It is also important when responding to these that you understand that the perpetrator probably has no idea they are in fact being offensive. While microaggressions will probably make you feel very angry, if you respond with anger the perpetrator will most likely be surprised and confused. Worse still, it might convey the idea that you are unstable or irrational as they don't realize they have been offensive. To respond effectively to microaggressions, it is important to ensure that you respond calmly but also that you state what the issue is.

You may get requests from people to support them or give advice. This can be really challenging but it is something that comes with advocacy. Once again, assertiveness is a good skill to have. It is also important to know your limitations. If you cannot provide a response or if the request is outside your area of knowledge, then say so. It is a good idea to make a list of experts in particular fields to whom you can refer people if you cannot answer their query. This can be people you know but it can also be neurodivergent bloggers or authors or others with a public profile.

There is a concept within the advocacy and activism world that neurodivergent people should not have to educate others. This is a good concept but sometimes education is actually an important part of advocacy. You can educate in a number of ways, including writing, speaking with individuals, and advocating for yourself. While these things are not a direct means of educating people, they are often an effective means of changing people's views. In fact, all the work of advocates can be seen as a kind of education – be they someone with an international profile or someone representing themselves when they have been discriminated against.

Advocating for those in your care

Sometimes you may be required to advocate for someone in your care, such as a child or partner. This is potentially quite a sensitive area. You want to enable the person to get the support they require and to get their needs met but you don't want to disempower them.

When advocating for others, it is essential to put their needs first. If they can communicate with you, discuss what they need and how they want you to support them. If they cannot communicate with you, use the 'golden rule' – do for them what you would want done for yourself in a similar situation. Even better, use what is called the platinum rule – do for them what they themselves would want (although if someone cannot communicate, this can be difficult).

Advocating for another person can be emotionally draining so make sure you get some downtime if possible. Remember that your advocacy could be making a huge difference for the person you care for.

Sometimes, advocating for someone else can put you in a position where people criticize or judge you. In fact, advocating for yourself often does this too! Keep in mind that you are doing a worthwhile thing and that the people who matter in the equation are the person you care for and you, not the critical, judgemental people. Often people lack empathy and understanding and judge without having any understanding of the situation. It can be hard navigating the world with critical people telling you how you are doing things wrong!

It can help to have support when you are advocating for someone. This could take the form of family members, friends, your partner, your kids, support groups or your family of choice. It helps to not have to walk your path alone. A lot of neurodivergent people struggle with assertiveness and asking for help. You might be surprised how supportive people can be if you just ask. However, not everyone will respond to a request for support positively so be prepared for that. If someone responds negatively, ask someone else.

It can be hard advocating for someone else when you require advocacy yourself! Neurodivergent parents, in particular, can have difficulties with needing advocacy themselves and also for their kids. This is where accessing support is absolutely critical. You should not have to do this alone – there are other sources of support such as online groups, friends, supportive family members or autism/ADHD/dyslexia groups.

Relationship between advocacy and activism

Many people wonder what the difference is between advocacy and activism. In fact, they share some elements and relate to each other. Activism tends to be more about making a point or a statement. An activist is more focused on effecting change, often significant change. Advocacy can be seen as more personal and about making change on a more individual level. Advocates can be self-advocates and/or systemic advocates. Systemic advocacy is similar to activism. The *Merriam-Webster* dictionary (2021) defines advocacy as 'the act or process of supporting a cause or proposal: the act or process of advocating something'. Activism is defined as 'a doctrine or practice that emphasizes direct vigorous action especially in support of or opposition to one side of a controversial issue'.

Activism tends to be viewed as more militant and hard-line than advocacy. However, there is overlap between the two – advocates can be activists, and activists can be advocates.

Is advocacy 'better' than activism?

Advocacy and activism both have a part to play in making change for neurodivergent people. It is not the case that advocacy is somehow 'better' than activism.

Dissent in the neurodiverse community

As in any community, there is dissent and disagreement within the neurodivergent community. Individuals can have arguments with others, and people or groups can be disrespectful or even engage in bullying behaviour. Neurodivergent people – and advocates – are human and therefore are prone to dissent and arguments. This does not make it okay and in a perfect world people would respect and support one another, but in reality that isn't always what happens.

As an advocate, you must try and rise above dissent and poor behaviour, even if it is difficult. It is important to remember that you are not in competition with others and that we do a lot better united than we do divided.

Case study: Yenn

A few years ago, there was an autism advocate who had a very public disagreement with another. I knew both of the people involved and felt very uncomfortable, especially as one of them was messaging me and instructing me to unfriend a load of people who were supporting the other person. I did not know what to do and felt very anxious. The person kept persisting in their demands that I unfriend people. In the end, I unfriended the person who had been insisting I remove people from my social media as I figured they were the one behaving poorly. The whole thing was very unpleasant and made me feel very uncomfortable. I still have nothing to do with that person and it is many years since the issues happened. I wish people would be more respectful and considerate. If we are trying to make the world a better place, we should probably start with our own behaviour!

Trolling

One thing that advocates – and everyone – can experience is trolling and bullying. This is particularly prevalent in social media but happens in other places too. Neurodivergent people may have experienced bullying at school as children, so this can be particularly traumatic and make them relive past trauma. Bullying and trolling are never the fault of the victim. The troll or bully is the one in the wrong but it can be hard to feel that is the case when you are on the receiving end of violence and abuse. Trolling can take the form of microaggressions, gaslighting, insults and name-calling. Seek support if you are experiencing bullying or trolling.

It is important to note that neurodivergent people can be bullies and trolls as well. This can be confusing and upsetting. Being neurodivergent does not automatically mean a person is going to respect other neurodivergent people.

If you are being trolled, try to connect with supportive people and tell someone it is happening. Remind yourself that the troll is in the wrong and not you. Being an advocate, particularly if you have a public profile as one, can make you a magnet for bullies and trolls. Sadly, standing up for what you believe in can attract the attention of negative people. Remind yourself that you are doing good things and the trolls are probably jealous of you for doing something worthwhile.

One strategy to address bullying is often helpful but can be difficult to do. This involves challenging the bully. Most bullies and trolls are cowards and their behaviour stems from feelings of inadequacy. If you meet them head on and challenge them, they will often back down. This is a difficult and potentially risky strategy, but it can be very helpful.

Conclusion

Elements of lasting change

The point of advocacy – be it the advocacy of the most popular public figure or the individual sticking up for themselves – is to change the world. This does not have to mean change on a global scale, although that would be good. Change can happen on an individual level, within families, schools or workplaces. Advocacy is about improving things for individuals and society. The point of advocacy is to make the world a little bit better. For example, creating:

- increased confidence among neurodivergent people
- improved relationships
- more understanding of the needs and experience of neurodivergent people
- more neurodivergent people in suitable work and study
- greater feelings of belonging
- better representation of neurodivergent people in media, business, government and so on
- less ableism/bullying.

Things have changed for the better in recent years, with more advocates and more opportunities for neurodivergent people, but there is still a long way to go. We need more advocates – systemic and individual. Everything we do in a positive direction makes a difference, whether it is Greta Thunberg advocating around environmental issues to a global audience, or an autistic parent advocating for their ADHD child to access supports at school.

Looking to the future

We have covered quite a bit about self-advocacy and self-determination and the many aspects that are involved in gaining these skills. These skills aren't something that you just learn from reading a book or doing an online course, they come from life experiences and having a good understanding of yourself.

By looking at these aspects that we have discussed within these pages, you can start identifying your needs, dreams and visions and bringing this information together to be the building blocks of strong self-advocacy and self-determination skills.

You will not learn these skills quickly. It is often a lifelong process as you continually learn more about yourself and encounter different life experiences. Each new experience adds to your toolbox of skills that you can use in similar situations or adapt to other situations.

As you begin to master these skills, it will help you with the most crucial situations in all aspects of your life. Topics covered in this book are some of the main features that help build stronger self-determination and self-advocacy skills.

Parents, employers, educators and allies who embrace a person-centred and a collaborative approach are putting neurodivergent people first and helping them to decide what they want for their lives.

When you gain these skills and feel supported and included, it is an incredibly empowering feeling. Having your value and worth validated, your supports, needs and accommodations provided through active listening, you are gaining the equal and right opportunities you deserve, just as every other person in society deserves.

So, what is the future for advocacy? We have seen an explosion of advocates in recent years, particularly autism advocates but for other neurodivergences too. This does not necessarily mean that things will keep travelling along a nice, neat trajectory. In this space, everything is up for grabs and we cannot be complacent. We need to see many more advocates, as the more of us there are, the better. We can't assume that things will keep improving. There are attacks on neurodivergent people all the time and these need to be addressed.

There are all sorts of different kinds of advocates and advocacy and that is a good thing. Everyone is helping. Whatever form your advocacy takes, if it is part of the efforts to make the world better, then that is good thing. We hope you found this book helpful. The aim of this book is to build the advocacy skills for neurodivergent people, be they public figures, parents, employees, young people or anyone else. The more the merrier when it comes to neurodivergent advocates. We wish you all the best in your advocacy journey.

Further reading

10 tips for being assertive (2021). Retrieved from www.betterhealth.vic. gov.au/health/HealthyLiving/assertiveness.

Activism (2021). Merriam-Webster. Retrieved from www.merriam-webster.com/dictionary/activism.

Advocacy (2021). Merriam-Webster. Retrieved from www.merriam-webster.com/dictionary/advocacy.

Block, P. (2015). 'The emergent landscape of autistic communities and autistic studies.' *Culture, Medicine, and Psychiatry*, 39(2), 351–355. doi: 10.1007/s11013-015-9453-8.

Bourhis, A. & Dubé, L. (2010). '"Structuring spontaneity": Investigating the impact of management practices on the success of virtual communities of practice.' *Journal of Information Science*, 36(2), 175–193. doi: 10.1177/0165551509357861.

Cassidy, S. & Rodgers, J. (2017). 'Understanding and prevention of suicide in autism.' *The Lancet Psychiatry*, 4(6), e11. doi: 10.1016/s2215-0366(17)30162-1.

Chown, N., Robinson, J., Beardon, L., Downing, J. et al. (2017). 'Improving research about us, with us: A draft framework for inclusive autism research.' *Disability & Society*, 32(5), 720–734. doi: 10.1080/09687599.2017.1320273.

Coleman, D. & Adams, J. (2018). 'Survey of vocational experiences of adults with Autism Spectrum Disorders, and recommendations on improving their employment.' *Journal of Vocational Rehabilitation*, 49(1), 67–78. doi: 10.3233/jvr-180955.

Fleischmann, A. (2014). *Carly's Voice*. New York, NY: Touchstone.

Fletcher-Watson, S., Adams, J., Brook, K., Charman, T. et al. (2018). 'Making the future together: Shaping autism research through meaningful participation.' *Autism*, 23(4), 943–953. doi: 10.1177/1362361318786721.

Fullan, M. (2001). *Leading in a Culture of Change*. San Francisco, CA: Jossey-Bass.

Kapp, S., Gillespie-Lynch, K., Sherman, L. & Hutman, T. (2013). 'Deficit, difference, or both? Autism and neurodiversity.' *Developmental Psychology*, 49(1), 59–71. doi: 10.1037/a0028353.

Kliewer, C., Biklen, D. & Petersen, A. (2015). 'At the end of intellectual disability.' *Harvard Educational Review*, 85(1), 1–85.

Kouzes, J. & Posner, B. (2003). *Encouraging the Heart*. San Francisco, CA: Pfeiffer.

Krcek, T. (2013). 'Deconstructing disability and neurodiversity: Controversial issues for autism and implications for social work.' *Journal of Progressive Human Services*, 24(1), 4–22. doi: 10.1080/10428232.2013.740406.

Kuhn, C.C., Nichols, M.R. & Belew, B.L. (2009). 'The Role of Humor in Transforming Stressful Events.' In T.W. Miller (ed.) *Handbook of Stressful Transitions Across the Lifespan* (pp.653–662). Lexington, KY: Springer.

Kumar, S., Tansley-Hancock, O., Sedley, W., Winston, J. *et al.* (2017). 'The brain basis for misophonia.' *Current Biology*, 27(4), 527–533. doi: 10.1016/j.cub.2016.12.048.

Kupferstein, H. (2018). 'Evidence of increased PTSD symptoms in autistics exposed to applied behavior analysis.' *Advances in Autism*, 4(1), 19–29. doi: 10.1108/aia-08-2017-0016.

Lane, A., Young, R., Baker, A. & Angley, M. (2009). 'Sensory processing subtypes in autism: Association with adaptive behavior.' *Journal of Autism and Developmental Disorders*, 40(1), 112–122. doi: 10.1007/s10803-009-0840-2.

MacLeod, A., Lewis, A. & Robertson, C. (2013). '"Why should I be like bloody Rain Man?!" Navigating the autistic identity.' *British Journal of Special Education*, 40(1), 41–49. doi: 10.1111/1467-8578.12015.

Nicolaidis, C. (2012). 'What can physicians learn from the neurodiversity movement?' *Virtual Mentor*, 14(6), 503–510. doi: 10.1001/virtualmentor.2012.14.6.oped1-1206.

Paradiz, V., Kelso, S., Nelson, A. & Earl, A. (2018). 'Essential self-advocacy and transition.' *Pediatrics*, 141(Supplement 4), S373–S377. doi: 10.1542/peds.2016-4300p.

Purkis, Y. (2014). *Wonderful World of Work*. London: Jessica Kingsley Publishers.

Purkis, Y. (2016). 10 Things ER Staffers Should Know About Autism. Retrieved from https://themighty.com/2016/07/things-er-staffers-should-know-about-autism.

Rose, J. (2017). 'The autism literary underground.' *Reception: Texts, Readers, Audiences, History*, 9(1), 56–81. Retrieved from www.jstor.org/stable/10.5325/reception.9.1.0056.

Senge, P. & Kleiner, A. (1999). *Dance of Change. Challenges of Sustaining Momentum in Learning Organizations. A Fifth Discipline Resource*. New York, NY: Doubleday.

Sinclair, J. (1993). 'Don't mourn for us.' Autism Network International Newsletter, *Our Voice*, 1(3). Retrieved from https://philosophy.ucsc.edu/SinclairDontMournForUs.pdf.

Singer, J. (2017). *Neurodiversity*. Amazon.

Sousa, A. (2011). 'From Refrigerator Mothers to Warrior-Heroes: The cultural identity transformation of mothers raising children with intellectual disabilities.' *Symbolic Interaction*, 34(2), 220–243. doi: 10.1525/si.2011.34.2.220.

Sullivan, J., Miller, L., Nielsen, D. & Schoen, S. (2014). 'The presence of migraines and its association with sensory hyperreactivity and anxiety symptomatology in children with autism spectrum disorder.' *Autism*, 18(6), 743–747. doi: 10.1177/1362361313489377.

Wenger, E., McDermott, R. & Snyder, W. (2002). *Cultivating Communities of Practice*. Boston, MA: Harvard Business School Press.